THE BUGIS CHRONICLE OF BONE

THE BUGIS CHRONICLE OF BONE

TRANSLATED AND EDITED BY
CAMPBELL MACKNIGHT, MUKHLIS PAENI
AND MUHLIS HADRAWI

PRESS

Published by ANU Press
The Australian National University
Acton ACT 2601, Australia
Email: anupress@anu.edu.au

Available to download for free at press.anu.edu.au

ISBN (print): 9781760463571
ISBN (online): 9781760463588

WorldCat (print): 1140933926
WorldCat (online): 1140933873

DOI: 10.22459/BCB.2020

Cover design and layout by ANU Press.

Cover image: The rice fields of Bone display the agricultural basis of the kingdom, while the lontar palms provided the original medium for Bugis writing (photograph by Campbell Macknight). The sword, La Téariduni, an item in the regalia of Bone, indicates military might. The chronicle records its name being used to represent the kingdom in a treaty from the middle of the sixteenth century (image from Perelaer 1872, vol. 2, plate 1).

Contents

Figures, maps and plates

Figures

Maps

Plates

Acknowledgements

The completion of this project has been unreasonably delayed. In 1975, in Leiden on study leave from The Australian National University, Campbell Macknight began to translate the version of the chronicle published by Matthes in his *Boegineesche Chrestomathie* (1864–72). This was at the suggestion and under the close supervision of the late Koos Noorduyn. Macknight gratefully acknowledges this assistance and all the help so freely offered by the Koninklijk Instituut voor Taal-, Land- en Volkenkunde (Royal Netherlands Institute of Southeast Asian and Caribbean Studies) and the Leiden University Library in the course of his repeated visits to Leiden. Jan Witkam in the past and Doris Jedamski more recently, together with their staff, have made working in the library's manuscript reading room a delight. The library has also supplied the images for Plates 1 and 2.

On a visit to Bone in 1978, Macknight was greatly helped by A. Muh. Ali Petta Nompo and other friends.

At the end of 1980, Mukhlis Paeni spent two months as a visiting fellow in the Department of History, Faculty of Arts, at The Australian National University in Canberra on a grant from the Australian Research Grants Committee. He and Macknight worked carefully through the Bugis transcription and English translation and it was at this time that we took the decision to focus on the NBG 101 version of the work. A first version of the Bugis transcription and translation was typed up. It is this version of the translation that has circulated among interested friends and has been much quoted in publications as Macknight and Mukhlis (forthcoming). We owe much to Shirley Bradley and Barbara Hutchison in the Department of History for their help at this time.

In the following years, Macknight used the translation in undergraduate teaching both at The Australian National University and at the University of Tasmania, as well as giving various seminars and conference papers on aspects of the work. Several key questions about the chronicle were addressed in articles, as detailed in the Introduction to the present volume. Macknight thanks all those students, discussants and editors who have helped to clarify and sharpen arguments. In particular, he is grateful for the long association with Ian Caldwell, first as a postgraduate student and then as friend, in the task of developing meaningful principles for Bugis philology.

Others who have helped in various ways over the years include David Bulbeck, Bill Cummings, Stephen Druce, Assa Doron, Elizabeth Macknight, the late Christian Pelras and the late Amin Sweeney.

In 2017, Muhlis Hadrawi came to the Department of Anthropology, School of Culture, History and Language, College of Asia and the Pacific, at The Australian National University as a visiting fellow. He revised the Bugis transcription and helped with the description of manuscripts.

For help in submitting the book to ANU Press, we are grateful to Jim Fox and, for eagle-eyed editing, to Jan Borrie.

Preface

The Bugis and Makasar historiography from South Sulawesi in Indonesia is a remarkable and highly distinctive tradition. Its major works from the seventeenth and eighteenth centuries allow us to understand how people of that time viewed the previous three centuries or so of their own past. These are not accounts by outsiders, such as we have from fragmentary Chinese records or travel narratives of European traders, but considered histories drawing on sources produced by the society itself.

The Bugis Chronicle of Bone is a major work within this tradition. It was written in the late seventeenth century—perhaps, as suggested later, in or soon after 1672—and has been widely known in South Sulawesi since then. There are many manuscript copies of the work. Some of the information in the chronicle has found its way into the scholarly literature on South Sulawesi and the text has been published several times in either Bugis script or transcription. There are also some whole or partial translations into Indonesian and Dutch. This is, however, the first edition to provide a reliable transcription of the Bugis text, a complete English translation and a discussion of various philological and historical issues.

Two general matters deserve comment.

The Bone chronicle fits clearly into the genre of works described as 'genealogical narrative texts' by Teeuw (1984) in his attempt to discern Indonesia as a 'field of literary study'. Within this genre, he discusses the Balinese *Babad Buleleng*, the Javanese *Babad Tanah Jawi* and *Pararaton*, the Malay *Sejarah Melayu*, *Hikayat Patani*, *Hikayat Raja-Raja Pasai*, *Hikayat Aceh* and *Hikayat Banjar dan Kotawaringin*; his only Bugis example is an eighteenth-century chronicle from Wajo. Most of the features of these texts that Teeuw sees as common across the genre can be found in the chronicle of Bone, such as the important role of genealogy and the determination of status, especially in the succession of rulers; the linkage between narrative and particular rulers; the supernatural elements in the origin of rule; and the 'open ending' of the work. Undoubtedly, he would have included both the Bone chronicle and the Makasar chronicles of Gowa and Tallo had satisfactory editions been available to him. As works of history and sources about the past, the South Sulawesi examples can certainly stand with these products of other Southeast Asian traditions.

Yet within the genre, the Bugis and Makasar works have a distinct tone. They display a directness that makes it easy to assume they are giving a 'realistic' view of the past, though, as will be shown later, there is rather more to be said about this in relation to the Bone chronicle. While there are certainly some supernatural events in the early stages of this narrative, as is common with other South Sulawesi historical traditions, such material serves a clear purpose in justifying the rule of those who can show appropriate descent. There is next to no interest in any religious ideas as such. Even in the account of the forced reception of Islam by Bone, which is highly unusual in the history of the expansion of Islam, the argument is cast in purely practical and political, rather than religious, terms.

The second matter for comment is the role the Bone chronicle and other Bugis and Makasar written sources from the seventeenth and eighteenth centuries, if not earlier, have already played in the dramatic new understanding of South Sulawesi history from about 1000 CE to about 1600 CE that has developed in the past few decades. The continuity of placenames, in particular, has allowed the integration of written sources and the results of extensive archaeological survey and excavation. South Sulawesi in the first half of the second millennium provides by far the best example of the evolution of an Austronesian-speaking society towards higher levels of political development in the almost complete absence of external influences. It throws comparative light on many parallel contexts across the Pacific, as well as in island Southeast Asia. The Bone chronicle with its emphasis on the selection and role of successive rulers is particularly useful in this regard. It is, in the end, a story about power.

The early history of South Sulawesi and even a critical history of Bone itself are not to be attempted here, but for any such undertaking, this chronicle provides abundant and essential material. It can also be read as a remarkably sophisticated account of the past, produced by Bugis society in the seventeenth century. As such, it takes its place among other major examples of Southeast Asian historiography.

Introduction

We present, in this book, a transliterated transcription of the Bugis text of the work known as the Chronicle of Bone, together with an English translation and notes. The chronicle deals with the affairs of this traditional kingdom in South Sulawesi—almost exactly in the centre of modern Indonesia—from the fourteenth century to the middle of the seventeenth century CE.

Our introduction provides the information needed for others to make use of the chronicle for their own purposes, whether these be historical, literary, linguistic or ethnological. We deal with the complex philological issues involved—for this is only one version of the work—and outline the cultural and historical contexts within which the chronicle was written.

1. The Chronicle of Bone in Bugis historiography

The richness and diversity of written materials in Bugis and Makasar, the main languages of South Sulawesi, were noticed by Leyden, Raffles, Crawfurd and other British scholars in the first half of the nineteenth century, but the works themselves were not properly accessible until the numerous publications of the Dutch linguist and Bible translator Benjamin Frederik Matthes in the second half of the nineteenth century. In his dictionaries, grammars, chrestomathies and, not least, catalogues of manuscripts, Matthes laid the foundations for later study.[1] His interests were remarkably wide and he collected manuscripts dealing with a vast range of subjects, particularly those dealing with the past.[2]

1 There is a convenient list of Matthes's published works in van den Brink (1943: 163–5).

2 Matthes also collected a great deal of literary material, especially the La Galigo narrative poems, as well as manuscripts dealing with theological, technical and cultural questions.

A.A. Cense has characterised and discussed various types of historical information found in Bugis and Makasar manuscripts. He distinguishes source materials—that is, diaries, treaty texts, *adat* legal records and correspondence—from historiographical literature in the form of short accounts of particular matters and chronicles. He also discusses the historical worth of various forms of verse, especially the *tolo'*, or Bugis narrative poetry with an eight-syllable line. Noorduyn, in the introduction to his edition of a chronicle of Wajo, lists other related material under the headings of chronicles, king lists, treaties and episodes. A further category is that of genealogies (Cense 1951; Noorduyn 1955).[3]

This chronicle sets out the succession of rulers in Bone, one of the major traditional kingdoms, from the first ruler—that is, the *tomanurung* or 'Descended one'—until the confused and traumatic events of early 1667. Apart from a brief introduction and a little material at the very end, all the information presented is structured within accounts of the reign of a particular ruler. Each account follows a pattern, with modifications as may be appropriate to the individual case: it proceeds through the ruler's relationship with the previous ruler and the circumstances of accession; his (or her) names, titles, marriages and children; the personal qualities of the ruler; noteworthy innovations during the reign; wars and other events of interest, including some quite detailed accounts of particular episodes; the circumstances of the ruler's testament and death; and, finally, his (or her) death name. Fortunately for the historian, the length of the reign is also given in most cases and a few synchronisms are possible, but there is no consistent attempt to relate events to any external or absolute system of dating.[4]

The relationship of the chronicles to the other categories of historical literature is apparent and, from occasional comments, we can even glimpse the process of the creation of the chronicles. For example, in the account of the family of the first ruler of Bone, after giving the names of two children important to the events of the next reign and specifying that there were five children in all, the chronicler continues: 'As for the other names [that is, those of the three unnamed children], they remain

3 Further discussions of this historiographical literature, or parts of it, may be found in Noorduyn (1961, 1965); Cense (1966); Abidin (1971); Hamonic (1980); Teeuw (1984); Macknight (2000); and Druce (2009). Tol (1990) is an excellent edition of a *tolo'*. Caldwell (1988) provides the text of some shorter works and, in a later article (1998), analyses some genealogies.

4 See Appendix 2 for discussion of absolute reign dates.

in records which are rolled up. This work only tells of the succession of events in Bone in their proper order.'[5] We do, in fact, possess materials that set out the names of all five children.[6] Genealogies often contain extensive information not set out in prose texts (Caldwell and Wellen 2016).[7] Similarly, when we are told that no tale has come down from the reign of Matinroé riBettung,[8] this probably means the chronicler had no episodes, to use Noorduyn's term, at his disposal, though the purely oral transmission of such stories is also possible. The only available details, other than the circumstances of that ruler's accession and death, were genealogical and the length of his reign. This suggests the possibility of derivation from a king list—again, using Noorduyn's term. There are many such lists for Bone, but none seems to be earlier than the chronicle and it is usually easier to derive the relevant sections of king lists from the chronicle than the reverse.[9] As Appendix 2 shows, however, this is not always the case and the chronicle is far from the sum of all we can discover from the sources about the history of Bone.

The chronicles are not, however, mere compilations of data. The author of the Bone chronicle has selected material with an eye to the overall purpose of tracing the succession of power in Bone. Thus, in the account of the first ruler's family mentioned above, the two children named are the second ruler, La Ummasa', and the mother of the third ruler, Kerrampélua'. Similarly, the more complicated genealogical matter in the account of the twelfth ruler, La Tenripale', looks forward to the role that several of those mentioned will play in later sections. On a deeper level, the account of the reign of the eighth ruler, La Icca', can be read as a justification for his murder and it is hard not to suspect some dramatic intention in the

5 See Chapter 1 in the chronicle. There are some minor differences between this version and the one found in Matthes (1864: 467), but these do not affect the general sense. Cense (1951: 54) gives a translation of this passage, but it is not clear on which version of the Bugis this is based.

6 Leid.F.Or.A9, p. 181, l. 5 up. (See Appendix 1 for details of this manuscript.) Blok (1817: Vol. 1, p. 36) also gives this information.

7 There is a very spectacular and extensive genealogy of the rulers of Bone held in the Leiden University Library collection (D Or. 295).

8 See Chapter 9 in the chronicle.

9 The most obvious is that appended by Matthes to his edition of the chronicle (1864: 499–501), though this also lists the rulers up to his own time in the middle of the nineteenth century.

story of the installation of the baby Kerrampélua' or the tale of the death of Boté'é. Although all the chronicles are concerned with the history of a particular polity, each has its own style and purpose.[10]

As well as the question of the date and circumstances of the production of the Bone chronicle, which are discussed in Section 8, there is the wider issue of the origin of the genre in Bugis and Makasar historiography, apparently in the seventeenth century. Macknight (2000) outlines aspects of the rich intellectual world from which the chronicles emerge. Many potential models, both religious and secular, in many languages could have stimulated an appreciation of historical method and the commitment to writing these relatively extensive narratives. Whatever influences may have been in play, however—whether Portuguese histories or Persian romances, Biblical stories or tales of the Prophet—the South Sulawesi chronicles are distinctive in the Southeast Asian context. As the discussion in Section 7 shows, the nature of the Bone chronicle bears close comparison with many European chronicles, even if no direct relationship can be established.

We have entitled the work published here *The Bugis Chronicle of Bone.*[11] Two issues are involved with this name. First, in sections 2 and 3, we turn to the question of whether we can distinguish a work in the sense of a unit properly amenable to editorial attention. This leads to a discussion of our editorial principles in sections 4, 5 and 6. Second, we deal, in sections 7 and 8, with the relationship of the work to the polity of Bone.

10 The Makasar chronicles of Gowa and Tallo—which may be regarded as a single unit—seem to be the earliest and are now available in Cummings's (2007) excellent edition. Noorduyn's (1955) edition of an eighteenth-century chronicle from Wajo includes, especially in its opening sections, material drawn from a variety of works, and the tradition of chronicle writing in Wajo continued into the twentieth century. Abidin (1985) provides much of another Wajo chronicle, originally from the eighteenth century. Both Noorduyn (1955) and Abidin (1985) list various versions of their central work and much other related material. The Tanete chronicle is a product of the late nineteenth century (Niemann 1883; Gising 2002). Caldwell (1988: vi) edits and translates several short works dealing with Soppeng, Sidenreng, Luwu and Cina, but as he observes, none of these amounts to a substantial chronicle. Druce (2009) also provides text and translation of some short works from the regions of Suppa' and Sawitto. Such short historical texts are found in great numbers, in both Bugis and Makasar, across the peninsula. Cummings (2002) provides translations of some Makasar examples.

11 The Bugis term *attoriolong*, which literally means 'an account of the people of earlier times', can be applied to various kinds of records of the past. It occurs only twice in this work and in both cases with reference to rolled up records in which further genealogical information can be found. It is also commonly used—but not in this work itself—to describe this work and a few other similar works, as discussed in the previous note. It is this sense of the term we translate as 'chronicle'. We further specify this as the 'Bugis chronicle' to avoid confusion with the English word 'bone' and as an aid to keyword searching.

2. The definition of the work

Most editors, even those working in a manuscript tradition, are able to define the object of their labours by means of a title and often identify an author. Not only is the corpus of Bugis historiography almost entirely anonymous, but, more fundamentally, the definition of any unit for editorial attention has to be established. It is in this sense that we use the term *work*. In other words, it is necessary to argue that the unit selected for editing represents a unit held at one time in the mind of its author (or authors).[12] This requires the assumption of deliberate creation or authorship, though it allows for the incorporation of earlier material. Even the original autograph of a work by its author may not represent quite what was in the author's mind, but the usual reality is that an editor has to deal with copies of the autograph at any number of removes. Leaving aside for the moment the question of variation arising from the process of copying in a manuscript register, we need to discern a work among the available manuscript materials.

Several arguments suggest that we are dealing with a work in this case. The most persuasive are the signs in the text itself of deliberate composition. The beginning sets out the subject of what follows—'the land of Bone and the ruling of Bone'—and indicates the method to be adopted, 'to set out in order the lineage of the ruling sovereigns'. The story starts at the beginning—that is, at the initiation of the polity, perhaps for the reasons discussed in Section 7. As the chronicle progresses, there is evidence for the selection of information and interrelationship between different sections of the account, as already discussed. Some weight should also be given to our subjective evaluation of the consistency of style and intent throughout the text.

Some indirect, but independent, support for regarding the chronicle as we have it as a work comes from consideration of the manuscripts themselves. As Appendix 1 shows, there are numerous examples of essentially the same text, to say nothing of the fragments of this text and other material derived from it. While one might still argue that the text comprises a collection of separate items that has become established as canonical, this view assumes a degree of reselection and rearrangement of

12 For a fuller discussion of the issue, see Macknight (1984).

material for which there is no evidence in this case. In other words, Bugis copyists have treated the present content—allowing for variations and some additions for particular purposes—as a unit.[13]

This leaves the problem of the abrupt end, which seems inappropriate for a consciously designed work. This issue is discussed in Section 8.

3. The manuscript

The chronicle of Bone is one of the most frequently copied works in the Bugis manuscript tradition. As explained in Section 4, we have chosen to present a diplomatic transcription of the Dutch Bible Society (Nederlands Bijbelgenootschap [NBG]) version in a single manuscript, known as NBG 101. A survey of some other versions of the work is provided in Appendix 1.

NBG 101

Dutch Bible Society (NBG) collection on loan to the Leiden University Library, Item 101. (There is a microfilm in the ANU Library.) The codex contains about 250 folios—that is, 500 pages—of European paper with Pro Patria and PB watermark and is bound in blue boards. The text terminates abruptly on page 248 and later pages are blank. Pages measure 32.5 x 20 cm, with a text written in a panel of 28 x 16.5 cm with 27 lines to the page. The text appears to be all by one hand and is written neatly in black ink on lines impressed from the recto of each folio. The *aksara* or characters are written continuously with no spaces between words, though some word divisions are marked by a *pallawa* or divider of three vertical dots. The scribe appears to have used a *kalam* or reed pen, rather than a metal nib. Several series of pagination occur, but the most useful page numbers are those written in large figures at the top left or centre of the pages. The contents are listed by Matthes (1875: 38–9). The chronicle text runs from the top of page 1 to the bottom of page 21. The first 12 pages of the text—that is, about half the chronicle of Bone—have been

13 Cummings (2007: 19), while agreeing on many of the causes of variation we describe for the Bone chronicle, takes a fundamentally different approach to the central issue for the Makasar chronicles: 'Though they began to be written in the late sixteenth century, the Gowa and Talloq chronicles were composed progressively. That is, upon the death of a ruler a new reign account was composed and added to the existing chronicle. Each such reign forms a coherent narrative unit, and there is nothing in the structure of the chronicles that necessitates they be viewed as a single whole composed at one sitting or by one writer.'

extensively annotated by Matthes and occasionally by others.[14] In these annotations, 'DM' (that is, Daeng Memangung) indicates NBG 99; 'Ar P' (Arung Padali) indicates NBG 100.[15] The annotations supply alternative readings from other manuscripts and the Dutch translation of difficult passages. Thereafter only the successive reigns in Bone are numbered.

From page 22, the codex contains the usual miscellany of items, dealing mostly with the history and affairs of Bone and other states. As Matthes notes in his listing of the contents, many items, including the chronicle of Bone, are shared with NBG 100 and the corresponding passages in other manuscripts are carefully referenced in the margin in a way that supports the description of the contents by Matthes.

At the front of the codex, after a blank flyleaf, there is a page with the following inscriptions: '"NB" over "N.101"', possibly in Matthes's hand; then, in another, very flowery, hand:

> Kronijk
> gevonden in de woning van de
> vorstin van Bonie Basse Kadjoe
> wara thans genaamd Aroe Pasem
> pa bij de imam van Pasempa
> op den 9 December 1859[16]

The codex was possibly obtained by J.A. Bakkers when Dutch troops looted the ArumPone's house at Pasémpe' on 9 December 1859 (Perelaer 1872: Vol. 2, p. 151). The role of the imam mentioned in the inscription is unclear. The codex was probably brought back to Europe by Matthes in 1870 (van den Brink 1943: 90). Relevant items are noted in Noorduyn's (1955: 21–31) list of material relating to Wajo.

4. The choice of this version of the work

In Section 2, we have defined a work as 'a unit held at one time in the mind of its author (or authors)'. The editor of such a work can choose one of two basic approaches to the material. A critical edition aspires to reconstruct the author's intention by purging the text—perhaps

14 For example, two annotations on page 6 are signed 'J.', which probably indicates J.C.G. Jonker.

15 Correspondingly, in those manuscripts, NBG 101 is indicated by 'B' for Bone.

16 'Chronicle found in the house of the queen of Bone, Bessé Kajuara, currently known as Arung Pasémpe', by the imam of Pasémpe' on 9 December 1859'.

even an autograph itself—of anything not the intention of the author. The alternative approach is a diplomatic edition, which seeks to provide an exact account of a restricted body of data—usually one manuscript. That is the approach we have chosen here.

The first option—that of a critical edition—is appropriate and reasonably possible in many situations. The vast scholarly effort expended over the centuries on Biblical texts is an obvious example of this approach and there are many others, ranging from scholarly editions of the works of Greek and Roman antiquity to our almost unconscious emendation of spelling mistakes in a friend's email message. The decision to follow the other approach—that of a diplomatic edition—requires explanation and justification.

The primary materials for the chronicle of Bone are found not merely in the manuscript register, but more precisely in the form of manuscripts in the Bugis tradition, including the script.[17] Macknight and Caldwell (2001) have argued that, while an awareness of philological and editorial practices generally is useful, procedures and expectations from other traditions are not necessarily applicable to the Bugis—and Makasar—manuscript tradition. It is not just that the South Sulawesi scripts are distinctive, but also the particular function of writing itself needs to be considered. One element of this is the reciprocal relationship between oral materials and written manuscripts as analysed by Pelras (1979).[18] In this context, it is easier to understand a relatively loose attitude to the integrity of texts, including historical works such as this, as they are copied or reworked from one manuscript to another. The interests being served by the act of copying are those of the owner of the codex into which the text is copied; very often perhaps, the owner was also the copying scribe. Little attention was given to protecting the 'moral rights' of the original author. At least, that is an impression derived from familiarity with a great many of the codices that make up the Bugis manuscript tradition as a whole,

17 The printed version in Matthes (1864) can be traced back directly to the manuscripts available to him—namely, NBG 99, NBG 100 and NBG 101. Later Romanised versions and translations discussed in Section 10 are taken either directly from Matthes's version or, it would seem, from a single manuscript.

18 There is much evidence for knowledge of the content of the work independent of a written text. The Bugis ambassador who supplied Raffles with an account of the early parts of the chronicle seems to have been able to do so orally (Raffles 1817: Vol. 2, pp. clxxix–xxxi). In 1978, A. Muh. Ali, then head of the cultural office in Watampone, was able to recall sections of the work without direct reference to a written text. In a Makasar context, Tideman (1908: 488–500) describes an oral account of the early history of Bajeng and notes particularly the absence of any manuscript on this occasion.

though there are some differences between genres. The consequence of this lack of respect for the integrity of the text combined with the widespread interest in this particular work is a plethora of texts exhibiting in full measure all the possibilities of variation described by Macknight and Caldwell (2001), ranging from minor differences in script to major reworking. This textual instability is compounded by our limited knowledge of early Bugis linguistic and literary conventions. We simply do not know enough to introduce stylistic suggestions with any degree of confidence. Any attempt to do so or to choose the textual detail of one manuscript rather than another ends up producing no more than yet another variant text of the work.

Yet the choice of which text to present is not quite as difficult as it might appear. To begin with, and as evident from the material described in Appendix 1, there are no major differences in content among a substantial number of versions. Moreover, in the absence of a stemma, we can be guided to some extent by extrinsic features of the manuscripts in which texts are found. NBG 101, which supplies the text for our transcription and translation, can be recommended on both intrinsic and extrinsic grounds.

The codex in which this version of the work is found came into Dutch hands in 1859. Although several other versions are known to have been in existence slightly earlier—such as the one known as Berlin 386, as described in Appendix 1—the middle of the nineteenth century is as far back as we can trace any of our present manuscript versions. In a few cases, we can determine a likely date for the actual copying of a codex, but more often, as for NBG 101, we have no means of estimating when exactly, between the manufacture of the paper and the collection of the codex, the copyist created the manuscript. Even if the abrupt ending of the text of NBG 101 on page 248 and the preparation of the following blank pages for writing suggest the text was being written shortly before the codex was collected in 1859, there may still have been a considerable time gap between the copying of the chronicle into the opening pages of the codex and the writing of page 248. It is enough to say that NBG 101 is among the oldest group of versions available.

More significantly, the codex was found on 9 December 1859 in the house at Pasémpe' deserted by the ArumPone in her flight from Dutch troops. The house, which had been abandoned precipitately, also contained a supply of rifles and considerable quantities of household effects. The

ArumPone took only objects of great intrinsic value and the regalia (Perelaer 1872: Vol. 2, pp. 149–51). While there is no need to assume the codex belonged to the ArumPone herself, if it did not, it was probably owned by a senior court official. The high degree of common content between this codex and that obtained in 1861 by Matthes from Arung Padali in Wajo—that is, NBG 100—shows that many items, including most of the text of this chronicle, were available in other noble circles (van den Brink 1943: 214). It is not surprising to find a slightly preferable version in Bone itself. The substantial break in the text of the chronicle in NBG 100, however, suggests a more complex relationship between the two versions than Noorduyn's (1955: 22) guess that his A5 in NBG 100 and his A6 in NBG 101 were very probably copied from the same model.

As Matthes (1875: 39) remarks in his catalogue, this manuscript is 'neatly and clearly written'. It also has the advantage of relative consistency of language and, as shown by the scarcity of notes to the text, few points of textual difficulty.

Given the decision to present a diplomatic edition, there is no other single version of the work with so much to commend it.

5. Principles of transcription

Two sets of issues arise when transcribing a Bugis text originally found in Lontara' characters into Latin characters. The first concerns the representation of the phonemes of the language and whether to divide up, in certain circumstances, the complexes or polymorphemic words that are such a feature of the language. Our policy on these issues is set out and exemplified in Macknight (2012). This amounts to an updated version of the system developed by Cense in the 1930s, as explained by Noorduyn in his edition of a Wajo chronicle (1955). It is also consistent with the system used by Sirk (1996).[19]

In summary, this involves giving the 18 consonants, and four prenasalised consonants, the values they have in modern Indonesian and rendering the glottal stop with an apostrophe –'– or before voiced occlusives as a geminated consonant, thus –'b– becomes –bb–. The glide –y– is omitted after –é– and –i–, and the glide –w– is omitted after –o– and –u–.

19 A minor variation is to write the first-person possessive suffix as –ku', rather than –ku.

The strong central vowel –é– is given an acute accent, while the weak vowel, schwa, has no diacritic mark, –e–. Polymorphemic complexes are not divided.

The second set of issues concerns the 'style' of transcription and transliteration. It involves questions specific to representing and transcribing a text written in the Lontara' characters used for Bugis and Makasar. Five 'styles' may be distinguished:

1. **Facsimile reproduction.** Strictly speaking, this involves neither transcription nor transliteration. Given modern methods of reproduction, this is easy to arrange, but has limited use for most readers. It is, however, the form, in the medium of microfilm, by which we have consulted the text of most of the manuscript versions of this work.
2. **Transcription of the Lontara' characters.** The Lontara' characters of an original manuscript text can now be rendered in letterpress printing or by modern computer fonts. Although not technically a transliteration, a transcription in this style may involve editorial decisions relating to word division, doubtful readings and punctuation, as well as judgements on the text itself. The text of the chronicle published by Matthes in the first volume of his *Boegineesche Chrestomathie* (1864: 465–98) is a good example of this style.
3. **Literal Latin style.** By assigning a fixed Latin character to each Bugis phoneme, it is possible to render the Lontara' characters with no ambiguity. It is, in effect, a literal transliteration. This can be useful when it is desirable to make easy reference to the original Lontara' characters, without any assumption as to how they should be read. The usual convention in this style is to use uppercase characters for consonants and lowercase for vowels, with the vowel-only syllable introduced by Q–. The first phrases of the chronicle would thus be rendered: Qi.Qa.Na.Qé.Su.Re.Po.Qa.Da.Qa.Da.Qé.NGi.Ta.Na. Qé.Ri.Bo.Né. This is unambiguous, but not very helpful for most purposes. It also allows the same editorial decisions as a transcription of the Lontara' characters.
4. **Expanded diplomatic style.** The remarkable efficiency of the Lontara' script for writing Bugis depends on omitting information necessary for a full realisation of the language—most notably, geminated consonants, some nasalisation to closed syllables and the glottal stop. A Latin transliteration that purports to be a useful version

of the original Bugis text must involve expanding the information in the Lontara' characters to make the language comprehensible and that is what we do in this edition. While moving from Lontara' to Latin characters involves some matters of editorial judgement, we have been meticulous in allowing the original text in Lontara' characters to be unambiguously reconstituted by the application of standard rules for removing editorial decisions. These rules are:

– All word divisions are editorial decisions.
– The *pallawa* or divider, which is the only punctuation mark in the Bugis text, is indicated by a vertical stroke –|–.
– Initial uppercase characters are used for proper names and to indicate the beginning of phrases and sentences. This avoids the need to add further punctuation and leaves more room for alternative constructions of the Bugis.
– All geminated consonants are editorial decisions.
– All glottal stops are editorial decisions.
– All nasalisations at the end of a syllable are editorial decisions, except where provided by prenasalised Lontara' characters. The use of these prenasalised characters is, however, inconsistent and, where appropriate but omitted, the nasalisation is added in pointed brackets, < >.
– The use of glides, or their frequent non-use where strictly required by the rules, is as indicated.

The effect of these editorial decisions is to produce a text that is both easily comprehensible and yet preserves the minor inconsistencies of the original. In practice, it is very similar to the following standard style.

5. **Standard style.** It has long been recognised that one consequence of Matthes's nineteenth-century publications on Bugis, especially his dictionary and grammar, has been to establish the language as spoken in Bone as the normative form. Other forms of speaking can be regarded as dialects. Following the conventions set out by Macknight (2012) and described above, it is possible to write Bugis using Latin characters, whether based on an original Lontara' text or, indeed, from transcription of the spoken language. This standard orthography has the merit of being effectively phonetic—that is, it accurately represents the spoken language and can, in turn, be read aloud as the spoken language. In particular, this style represents the effects of elision or sandhi—that is, the phonetic results of running

morphemes together to produce complexes of various kinds. The most common instance arises from the combination of the title *Arung*, meaning ruler, and a following placename. Thus, in standard style, *Arung* + Palakka is written, as it is pronounced and as the original Lontara' characters indicate, *ArupPalakka*. Like the diplomatic style, it is possible to work from the Latin characters in the standard style back to Lontara' characters without ambiguity, though the *pallawa* is not usually indicated—and that, in either writing system, represents the formally correct spoken language.

6. **Hyper-correct style.** This is essentially a style based on individual morphemes without taking account of their combination in the spoken language. It divides up some of the complexes and this makes their component parts more easily recognisable. Thus, it writes the elements of a personal title separately, as Arung Palakka.

6. Principles of translation

No translation can satisfy every requirement that may be made of it. In offering this translation, therefore, it is as well to set out the purposes, and audiences, we have had most clearly in mind. These purposes have determined the principles of translation. But Bugis is not an easy language to translate.

In the first place, the translation presents as complete a statement as possible of our understanding of the meaning of the Bugis text. Given the differences in the structure of Bugis and English and the remarkable compression of meaning in many Bugis complexes, it has been difficult to achieve a completely natural English style. Given the linguistic interest in an extended Bugis text and the relative lack of English translations of such material, we have not shied away from a slight tendency to pedantry. Words and phrases in parentheses, ( ), are amplifications or explanations not directly justified by anything in the Bugis text.

Our second purpose has been to provide a translation that will be accessible to those readers who know no Bugis. We have kept Bugis terms in the translation to a minimum and provided explanation of those used, especially those personal names that have a clear and relevant meaning in Bugis. With personal names, however, it is not possible to avoid using the Bugis name or, in some later cases, the Arabic name. This does not apply to the names of familiar places for which, in the English translation, we use the contemporary Indonesian version of names, even when this is inconsistent with the Bugis form. Thus, we write Gowa, Wajo and Luwu (rather than Goa, Wajo' and Luu') and Bone without an acute accent on the final vowel. For the unfamiliar names of minor villages, we retain the Bugis form.

One term requires particular comment. Despite the danger of cultural misunderstanding, we have translated *arung* where it appears independently as 'king' or 'queen', depending on the sex of the individual, and kept the same equivalence in other forms such as 'kingship' for *akkarungeng*. Where *arung* is followed immediately by a placename, we have treated it as a title, as in Arung Ujung, with the placename in its Indonesian form. Frequency of use and familiarity with the standard style of transcription and transliteration excuse the slight exception of writing ArumPone, rather than 'Arung Bone' or the Bugis forms 'Arung Boné' or 'Arumponé'.

7. The nature of the work

The interpretation of a written source necessarily involves assumptions about the nature of the text in question. What did the author understand to be the nature of the work? In Section 1, we have described the work, within the body of Bugis historiography, as a chronicle. The question is, however, more general than that of genre and, in any case, we know far too little about older Bugis literature to be able to characterise genre with any assurance. Similarly, our inquiry need not be confined to the original function or purpose of the work, about which we have no external information at all, for we can consider later functions as well. Assuming we have a version of the work reasonably close to that in the mind of its creator, the most reliable evidence on the nature of the work will be internal; it will come from analysing the text itself.

An issue that presents itself immediately is orality. Over recent decades, scholars have increasingly recognised that virtually all premodern writing in the Indonesian Archipelago—and far beyond—was intended primarily to be heard. To anyone familiar with Malay materials, for example, the statement in the opening paragraph of the chronicle that it is 'for hearing' seems unexceptional. There is no cause to doubt the literal sense of 'telling' in the word *ripau* used later in respect of the work.

Yet the work is clearly not oral in the terms of either of the two main understandings of orality in recent scholarship. That is, first, there are no traces of oral composition, such as standard epithets, formulaic passages and repetition. In the classic discussion of oral composition (Parry 1971), these features are related to verse rather than prose, but the general thrust of the argument suggests that an orally composed prose style (if such be possible in this context) is far removed from the rather jejune style of the chronicle. Second, and more importantly, the work is not primarily a 'tribal encyclopaedia' in the sense of that phrase used by Havelock (1963). The central point of Havelock's argument is to distinguish between two mental attitudes—one committed to the implicit truth of memorised material, the other able to compare alternative accounts to analyse a subject. Whether a performer has the material to perform through a process of oral composition or as a result of memorising, in neither case is there any possibility of comparing accounts, and the values expressed in the performance relate necessarily to those of the audience—that is, they provide models and norms of behaviour for society.[20] As already discussed in sections 1 and 2, however, there is evidence within the text of the chronicle for the selection of material, including written sources, and the deliberate omission of material; this displays a quality of judgement quite impossible, according to Havelock, for a work limited to a purely oral context. If this applies to the work's creation, we may assume it tells us something about the context within which the work was to be first used.[21] The initial audience for the work was, presumably, capable of appreciating the selection and discrimination between sources.

It would be possible to resolve the contradiction between the expressions of an aural and oral element in the initial intention of the work and the evidence of considered judgement found in the text itself by asserting that the words and phrases relating to hearing and telling are merely conventional and should not be taken literally—that is, they derive from earlier genres of storytelling. There may be some truth in that approach, but it seems insufficient.

20 The contrast could not be sharper between the various genres of Bugis historiography, including the chronicles, and the huge corpus of stories in the La Galigo cycle. For a discussion of the La Galigo material as oral composition, see Macknight (2003), and as tribal encyclopaedia, see Koolhof (1999).

21 This does not preclude later use of the work involving more or less precise memorisation as described in Note 17. Such memorisation may represent no more than knowledge of Bone's history, rather than reliance on the work as a 'tribal encyclopaedia'. We can also set aside the question of an oral rendition of the work in the process of creating a manuscript copy of the work, as this is essentially a secondary and technical phenomenon (Macknight and Caldwell 2001).

Another approach to this problem has been developed by Christian Pelras with, very fortunately, specific reference to Bugis materials. In a paper with important implications for many literary traditions, Pelras (1979) has examined the oral performance of several kinds of written texts. His central purpose is to show the equality of esteem and the mutual interaction of writing in manuscript form and oral performance across several present-day Bugis literary genres. He does not deal with historiographical materials such as chronicles, nor should we unquestioningly transfer his modern observations to some period in the past, but his examples of an oral performer's additions and explanations when performing a manuscript text suggest ways in which a text such as the chronicle might have been transformed in oral performance. It is critical to note that the written text is in the manuscript register; it is not printed. The introduction of printing introduces another level of dissociation between the oral and the written. Once free of any higher estimation of the written text over the oral, and remembering the limited readership of any single manuscript, it is even possible to push the argument a little further. For a work created to achieve some public effect—and, as we suggest below, that is a reasonable claim for the chronicle—an oral performance of some kind is required to realise the author's intention, even if the detailed circumstances and oral text of that performance or performances necessarily remain unclear. This introduces the question of the purpose of the work insofar as that may be determined on internal evidence.

Noorduyn has remarked that 'South Celebes historical writing is characterized by a certain terseness and matter-of-factness' (1965: 140). He refers to this chronicle, among other works, in support of this proposition and it is easy to find illustrations of the qualities he is describing. One might refer, for a relatively straightforward example, to the account of the fourth ruler, Makkalempié, at the beginning of the sixteenth century. We learn that she succeeded her father, that she also held other territory and that she was 'praised as having intelligence'. Then her marriage is recorded and the names are given of the only two of her nine children relevant to the concerns of the chronicle. The record of agricultural expansion, including a brief war, leads into details of the career of these two sons, her abdication in favour of one of them and, after she moves to live with the other, a brief account of the legend of her disappearance. A similar process of selection—sometimes for particular reasons, as discussed further below—applies to the greater part of the work and is enough, in itself, to suggest it would be unwise to accept the chronicle as a mere catalogue of data. The need for such caution overall is confirmed by two other general features: the self-consciousness of the authorship and the 'realism' of the style.

We have argued above that the work is a conscious creation. Our previous purpose was to define the work and relate it to other forms of Bugis historiography, but we can now see another consequence of this self-consciousness. Any work that is deliberately produced and is more than a chance combination of information will have some model and some purpose. We may not be able to fully specify either the genre or the function of a particular work, but that does not mean the work was produced without precedent or purpose.

A second feature of the chronicle's style is its 'realism'. The text purports to describe actual events. In the celebrated first chapter of his book *Mimesis* (1953), Erich Auerbach develops the contrast between the Homeric poems that do not, in themselves, demand literal belief—whatever position one may take on the poems' actual use to the historian—and the early books of the Hebrew scriptures, which do purport to describe actual events. Yet it is just this comparison between the chronicle and the Hebrew scriptures that suggests caution. The intention of the creators of these early books of the Bible would seem to be to demonstrate divine concern with human affairs and to specify the appropriate human response. Reduced to essentials, this is no more than the familiar claim that history provides a guide for the present and the future. This claim requires, of course, a reliable record of the past and that implies a 'realist' style.[22] There is no reason to doubt the force of this logic in the Bugis, as in the Western, tradition.

This self-consciousness and realist style do not mean we should accept the account of the past that the chronicle offers as true. Indeed, one could argue these qualities are just what should alert our suspicion; what line are we being sold? Our author may be prepared to qualify his belief in the historicity of, say, the mysterious disappearance of the fourth ruler, Makkalempié ('She who disappeared in Cina'), but that implies the veracity of other information. Perhaps we should not accept the implication.

22 The argument is not invalidated by the literal belief accorded some literary works, such as the Homeric poems or even the La Galigo stories, at some times and in some places. This false belief arises from mistaking a literary text for a historical source. Even the use of a literary work as a 'tribal encyclopaedia' or exemplar of values can apply only to the period of the work's creation, or at least as imagined to be appropriate by the work's creators. Literary works such as historical novels do not, in themselves, provide evidence for the values of an earlier period in which a narrative may be set.

Such scepticism is excessive. There is no reason to doubt the essential reliability of the chronicle's account of most of the events described. For the events at the very end of the last section involving the Dutch, there is abundant supporting evidence in European sources and, from about the reign of the seventh ruler, Bongkangngé, in the middle of the sixteenth century, if not earlier, the Bone account is corroborated by corresponding material from Gowa and other kingdoms. Even in the information from the earliest reigns, there is a geographical logic that can be discerned through the lists of territorial conquest and alliance.[23] We need not, of course, believe that every word of direct speech is a verbatim account of what was said on a particular occasion, and perhaps the author of the chronicle could remark with Thucydides that

> my method has been, while keeping as closely as possible to the general sense of the words that were actually used, to make the speakers say what, in my opinion, was called for by each situation. (Thucydides 1.22, in Warner 1954: 24)[24]

Both we and the chronicle's author are left with a more difficult problem: the supernatural elements at the beginning of the work. The sources for the early chapters apparently included certain episodes or stories that seem to us to be difficult to explain in the context of normal human experience. That they appeared in the same light to the author is shown by his use of the word *garé'* (translated as 'so the story goes') or other disclaimers such as *riasengngi* ('it is said'). A clear example is the tale of the disappearance of Makkalempié at the end of Chapter 4. Cense (1951: 55) has drawn attention to a slightly fuller version of this story among a collection of episodes dealing with early Bone.[25] Comparing the two passages, one finds not only some editing by the author of the chronicle, but also the insertion of two *garé'*. The word is used three times in the description of the enthronement of Kerrampélua' as a baby and subsequent arrangements. It also appears right at the beginning of the *tomanurung* episode, where it is quickly followed twice by *riasengngi*. Given the overall 'realist' style of the work, how is the inclusion of these episodes to be understood?

23 Macknight (1983) has exploited this logic to trace the expansion of wet rice agriculture.

24 Thucydides 1:22 in Warner (1954: 24).

25 This is to be found at pages 173–223 in Leiden F.Or.A9 following a version of the chronicle itself. The passage translated by Cense (1951: 55) is at page 202, lines 2–7. Cense's suggestion that the author of the chronicle had edited the story with Muslim sensibilities in mind may be true, but it is not a necessary conclusion. It should be noted that the version of the chronicle found earlier in this manuscript has only one *garé'* in the relevant passage (p. 152).

In approaching this problem, we need to recall that the chronicle is not a single narrative unit. As explained in Section 1, it is a series of accounts of successive reigns or, to put the point more generally, accounts of ruling. This is, after all, how the work announces itself: 'This work tells of the land of Bone and the ruling of Bone.' The relevance of this point to the end of the work will be discussed in the next section, but here we are concerned with the earlier chapters. At the risk of oversimplifying what might have been a rather complicated process, we can see how this structure of accounts of successive reigns has been filled out in the earliest reigns with certain material, some of which raises 'realist' doubts. The most notable example, of course, is the story of the appearance of the *tomanurung* at Matajang, which takes up much of the first chapter. No details are given about the appearance of his wife, the *tomanurung* at Toro', but we are left to assume an equally supernatural process. Other examples of the supernatural can be seen in the explanations of the titles or non-personal names by which the early rulers are known: the first ruler, the *tomanurung*, was known only as Matasilompo'é, or 'The Eye of the whole plain', because he could judge the number of his people or perhaps because he could see all the territory he controlled; the second ruler, La Ummasa', is described as To Mulaiépanreng, or 'He who first had a grave', to emphasise the point that his parents disappeared without a grave; the name of the third ruler, Kerrampélua', refers to the detail that his hair stood on end at his birth, though the whole story of his early life is intensely realistic; his successor, Makkalempié, acquired the name Mallajangngé riCina, or 'She who disappeared in Cina', directly as result of her mysterious death. This theme of descent from on high and continuing contact with the supernatural carries the implication of high status and is found widely across South Sulawesi. A *tomanurung* figure stands at the head of most genealogies across the peninsula, sometimes linked with a *totompo'* figure who has risen from the waves.[26] A striking feature of these stories is that the high status of these figures is recognised beyond the particular community they come to rule. That means the high status of the descendants of any *tomanurung* can be acknowledged when seeking a marriage partner.

26 Caldwell and Wellen (2016) deal with this theme and, especially, its Malay expression.

The stories also connect with two themes found widely across Austronesian-speaking societies. The first is the cosmological structure of upper, middle and lower worlds. High-status beings from the upper world, or sometimes the upper world and the lower world, come together to initiate status and all that goes with it in the middle world. Nowhere is this more clearly described than in the Bugis La Galigo cycle, which begins with, in effect, its own *tomanurung* story, but the theme is found in many variations in other societies (Macknight 2003). The second theme is that of the stranger king where an outsider is needed to establish the status hierarchy, though usually in association with some local power as well.[27]

For the author of the chronicle—or some unknown predecessor, since there is no reason to suppose the chronicle was the first work to take this step—the supernatural elements in the early chapters serve two purposes. First, they provide some content for the account of the early rulers, even if that requires a disclaimer. More importantly, the association with the supernatural justifies the assumption of rule. Kern (1929: 297) writes of the gods providing 'letters of nobility [*brieven van adeldom*]'. This can be restated more generally as explaining the concept of ascribed status. The elaboration of the 'people's' role in accepting the *tomanurung* as their ruler is significant in this argument. Their acceptance is an acknowledgement of the validity of the first ruler's status.

There is a sense in which the whole chronicle is about status. The genealogical details for each ruler demonstrate his or her links with the *tomanurung* as a class and hence the correct ascription of status. The events of each reign show the operation of this status. Nowhere is this more apparent than in the account of the madness of the eighth ruler, La Icca'. The final justification for his killing is the claim that 'he is no king'—that is, he has forfeited his status. The incorporation of these supernatural elements—above all, the *tomanurung* story—into the structure of the chronicle provides an answer to the central question: what is the nature of rule, or power, in Bone? The ideological answer—as distinct from the political answer—is that some people are born to rule.[28]

27 Among the articles in the special issue of *Indonesia and the Malay World* devoted to stranger kings in Indonesia and beyond (Vol. 36, No. 105, July 2008), the most relevant are Fox (2008) and Henley and Caldwell (2008).

28 For the mechanisms by which ideology is adapted to reality—or reality to ideology—see the brilliant ethnography of Millar (1989). There are abundant traces of comparable processes at work in Bugis society at all periods for which we have records.

It would be too simple, however, to claim that the chronicle serves merely to justify the status quo. For one thing, we would need to know much more about the particular political circumstances at the time of the work's creation before being able to make such an assertion and, second, we would need to have some idea of the circumstances in which it was designed to be heard. On neither of these issues is there reliable information. The next section offers some speculation.

8. The date of the work and the problem of the end

In Section 2, we argued that the chronicle is, essentially, a unified work. Thus, although it undoubtedly incorporates information from earlier materials, the work in the form we have it cannot pre-date the latest events described. Fortunately, the events on Butung recounted at the very end of the chronicle can be firmly dated by reference to other records. The defeat of Karaeng Bontomarannu and the army of Gowa, including a forced contingent from Bone, took place over the first four days of 1667. Not only are there the vivid and detailed Dutch records of the great expedition against Gowa under the command of Cornelis Speelman—which include much information on Arung Palakka's activities and contact with the troops from Bone pressed into Gowa's service (Stapel 1922: 105–9; Andaya 1981: 76–8)—but also the date of Karaeng Bontomarannu's surrender on 3 January is confirmed in a Gowa diary (Cummings 2010: 101) and the Malay poetic account of the war gives some insight into the attitude of the Gowa court (Skinner 1963: 99–105). No event could be more securely fixed in time.

If that is the earliest possible date for the composition of the work, the latest possible date is the early nineteenth century. In 1814, John Crawfurd collected in Sulawesi 'several native writings, both in Bugis and Macassar language, of which translations were made into Malay for the author's use. The originals are in his possession' (Crawfurd 1820: Vol. 2, p. 390n.). Although no Bugis text of the chronicle is included among the many Crawfurd manuscripts now in the British Library, a Malay translation demonstrates that he once had access to a version.[29] The presence of the

29 British Library, Department of Oriental Manuscripts and Printed Books, Add. 12396, in Ricklefs and Voorhoeve (1977: 109).

chronicle in other manuscripts collected in the first half of the nineteenth century confirms its widespread distribution at that time. Thus, the Berlin 386 manuscript came from the collection of the well-known German scholar A.W. Schlegel, who died in 1845. The Schoemann VII, 4 manuscript, also in Berlin, which contains a substantial fragment of the chronicle, seems to have been collected in 1849, while Matthes was collecting or commissioning manuscripts now in the Dutch Bible Society collection in Leiden from his arrival in Makassar in 1848 onwards.

Having set those outer limits, as it were, how can they be narrowed? One attractive, but probably misleading, argument needs to be confronted. Two individuals who died after 1667 are referred to by their death names. The most important—he could hardly be more important—is Arung Palakka, Matinroé riBontoala', who died on 6 April 1696 (Andaya 1981: 296; Cummings 2010: 167). The other is La Maddaremmeng, Matinroé riBukaka, who died on 5 August 1678 (Cummings 2010: 136). Both death names are mentioned several times towards the end of the chronicle and one might argue that this means the work could not have been written before 1696. The weakness with this argument is the prominence of the two men involved. A later copyist, knowing the overall format of the regnal entries, could easily have added in such well-known names or substituted them for others. This is exactly the kind of minor content variation that occurs very frequently between manuscript versions of a Bugis work (Macknight and Caldwell 2001).

Another line of approach is to look for references to the work in a source dated before the middle of the nineteenth century and thus establish an earlier date by which the work must have existed. The difficulty with this argument is that, although there is some evidence of the history of Bone being known to Europeans from the time of Speelman on, as set out in the next section, such information does not necessarily imply access to this particular work. The information could have come from other historical works, including those sources used in the creation of the chronicle. That is not to say, of course, that it is not highly likely that the chronicle, as we have it, did exist in the eighteenth century; we just cannot demonstrate that conclusively.[30]

30 The extensive genealogy of the Bone rulers held in the Leiden University Library (D Or. 295) appears to date from the eighteenth century and is headed by an extensive quotation from the opening passage of the chronicle up to the marriage of Matasilompo'é. This suggests, unsurprisingly, that the work was known before 1800, but the date of the source is not certain.

To go further involves a degree of speculation, but the interest of the matter justifies the attempt. Two tenuous lines of argument suggest that the work, in the sense defined in Section 2, was created at some point within the last three decades of the seventeenth century—that is, between about 1670 and 1700.

The first argument arises from looking more generally at the historiographical tradition of South Sulawesi. Within the category of chronicles, the examples most similar to the chronicle of Bone are the Makasar chronicles of Gowa and Tallo, which, it is argued, are intimately related to each other (Cummings 2007: 21–3). The Makasar works demonstrate much interest in genealogical matters—rather more, in fact, than the Bone chronicle shows.[31] In this context, however, the similarities of the works are more relevant: they are all divided into reigns; they all begin with some apparently legendary material before lapsing into the 'realist' style; and all end in the seventeenth century without describing the cataclysmic events associated with the wars of the late 1660s. There is a clear stylistic difference between these three works and the more discursive narratives of the eighteenth-century Wajo chronicle edited by Noorduyn (1955) and much other material from Wajo (Abidin 1985). Much shorter works, such as those from Luwu or Soppeng, which are sometimes described as 'chronicles', turn out to be essentially legendary material and probably date from after 1700 CE (Caldwell 1988).[32] Whatever the interest of these minor works, any comparative dating of the Bone chronicle can be limited to comparison with the material from Gowa and Tallo.

Cummings (2007: 24), in his careful discussion of the manuscript versions of the Gowa and Tallo chronicles, states that with the death of Sultan Hasanuddin in 1670, 'chronicle composition ceased' and Cornelis Speelman, the leader of the Dutch in the wars of the 1660s, described versions of those two chronicles in his *Notitie* of 1670 (2007: 21).[33]

31 This point is also made by Noorduyn (1961: 33).

32 See Section 1.

33 Cummings sees the manuscripts with which he is dealing as representing the end of a tradition of chronicle writing. He says that 'though they began to be written in the late sixteenth century, the Gowa and Talloq chronicles were composed progressively' and 'the sheer variety of endings is evidence that multiple manuscripts existed that were based on originals composed at different points during the seventeenth century' (Cummings 2007: 19). We see the Bone chronicle as essentially a singular creation because of its many internal consistencies, though the author has obviously made use of prior sources and some of the many variant forms of the work in the manuscripts indicate the particular interests of later copyists.

Cummings stresses the genealogical character of the Gowa and Tallo chronicles; moreover, he believes 'this genealogical character was politically significant' and 'the genealogical-infused chronicles are social maps of the extent and substance of the realm' (Cummings 2007: 11). Elsewhere, Cummings (2002) has laid out in detail the relationship he sees between writing and ascriptive status. At least in general terms, it seems reasonable to associate the production of chronicles with the expansion and apogee of the political power of Gowa and Tallo in the mid-seventeenth century.

The Bone chronicle can be seen, in a sense, as a response to the Gowa and Tallo chronicles, or as emulation of them. There were certainly plenty of opportunities for young nobles from Bone, especially Arung Palakka, to observe the ways of the Gowa and Tallo courts before the wars of the late 1660s (Andaya 1981: 51). The Bone chronicle, however, is more focused than its presumptive models. The less expansive genealogical compass is carefully directed towards the succession of rulers, rather than the nobility of the whole realm. Moreover, from the account of the reign of the ninth ArumPone, La Pattawe', in the late sixteenth century, the ground is prepared for justifying the succession of Arung Palakka in 1672 by recording the marriage of his grandfather La Tenrirua, later the eleventh ArumPone, and his grandmother Dangke', followed by the birth of his mother, Wé Tenrisui. Later, in the account of the reign of La Tenripale', Matinroé riTallo', the twelfth ArumPone in the early seventeenth century, this is followed by setting out the names of his mother, the ArumPone's sister, and of his father and other children in the family. Given the Bone chronicle cannot be earlier than 1667, as explained above, and Cummings's date for the Gowa and Tallo chronicles is not after 1670, it is an attractive suggestion that the Bone chronicle reflects the circumstances of a period when Arung Palakka was ArumPone—that is, between 1672 and his death in 1696—or at least when his influence was strong.

A second argument leads to the same conclusion. Most of the complete manuscript copies end with the events on Butung in 1667; that seems to be the conclusion of the work in the sense used above. How is this abrupt ending to be explained? Consider what might follow. Given the structure of the chronicle, it would be necessary to begin the account of Arung Palakka's reign as ArumPone. If he were still the reigning ArumPone, there would be obvious difficulties in attempting the normal treatment of the reign by topics. Yet, as just explained, the author is even more aware of the importance of Arung Palakka than his substantial achievements until 1667 might suggest.

There is a further, more subtle, point. The chronicle makes it appear as though nothing further of relevance to the history of Bone was effected by La Maddaremmeng, Matinroé riBukaka, after he was defeated, captured and sent into exile in Siang. There, 'he was no longer king of Bone' and the account that follows appears to cover an interregnum until the end of the chronicle. This is a very partial account indeed. The Gowa diary tells us he was brought to Makassar on 23 July 1644 (Cummings 2010: 63). Nearly two years later, on 19 June 1646, he was sent to Siang after the Gowa ruler had returned from defeating Bone again at Pasémpe' (Cummings 2010: 66). Then, on 7 February 1667, he was taken to Bone and reinstalled as ArumPone (Cummings 2010: 101) until, apparently, forced to abdicate in favour of Arung Palakka in 1672. He did not die until 1678 (Cummings 2010: 136). He was buried at Bukaka on the outskirts of Watampone, which suggests he was living nearby at that time. Although La Maddaremmeng is the last person in the chronicle whose name is preceded by the phrase 'may my belly not swell'—since he had after all been ArumPone for 15 years before 1644—the failure to mention his second period of rule from 1667 to 1672 is striking. Perhaps Arung Palakka refused to recognise this reinstallation as valid. Such underplaying of La Maddaremmeng's career only casts Arung Palakka's achievements in a more favourable light.

There is a particular juncture when it would have served the interests of Arung Palakka to be presented as an appropriate and even necessary ArumPone. Although the details are obscure, La Maddaremmeng seems to have hoped that his son, La Pakkoko'é, would succeed him as ArumPone and, when that did not eventuate, La Pakkoko'é and other disaffected interests mounted a serious rebellion in late 1672 and early 1673 (Andaya 1981: 148–51). It may be relevant to remember here that Arung Palakka was childless, despite having many wives. In a context where Arung Palakka was seeking recognition and legitimisation, the chronicle as we have it places him firmly in the long series of those who have ruled in Bone. Whether or not one can tie the usefulness of the chronicle closely to Arung Palakka's struggle with La Maddaremmeng and his party in 1672, an early date in the reign seems more likely than a later date for the creation of such a work.

9. Early Western-language comment on the events of the chronicle

Bone and its history only came to have significant relevance to the affairs of Europeans in the Indonesian Archipelago during the 1660s, when it became mutually advantageous for Arung Palakka and those who followed him to join with the Dutch East India Company forces in military operations—first, on the west coast of Sumatra and then, second and more importantly, in the eventual overthrow of Gowa and its allies in South Sulawesi. Although Dutch interest in the peninsula remained chiefly focused on the southwestern area until the beginning of the twentieth century, the Dutch relationship with Bone largely determined the pattern of politics and no general account of the area can pass over Bone. Most of the writers offering such an account have something to say about Bone's history, but one must distinguish carefully between comment based on the work presented here—that is, the chronicle in this form—and a more general knowledge of names and events. This general knowledge often reflects contact with educated Bugis who probably had access not only to oral sources, but also to other forms of historical writing about Bone.

The earliest of these accounts is the *Notitie* of Cornelis Speelman, the commander of the Dutch East India Company's forces in the 'eastern quarters' between 1666 and 1669. This lengthy document, which was presented to his superiors in Batavia on 17 February 1670 (Stapel 1936: 72–4), contains a wealth of detail on many matters concerning South Sulawesi.[34] Speelman deals with each of the peninsula's states in turn, coming to Bone after Luwu. He comments specifically that he lost certain notes.[35] His account begins just before the middle of the sixteenth century—that is, more than a century before his own time—with the alliance of the sixth ArumPone, Boté'é, and the ruler of Gowa, Tumapa'risi' Kallonna, against Luwu. The account that follows brings the narrative up to the 1640s.[36] There is nothing in this account that requires knowledge of the chronicle and much that must come from elsewhere. Indeed, a few details suggest a lack of knowledge of the chronicle. For instance,

34 Noorduyn (1983: 100–1) describes the various surviving copies of this document. In the following references, we use the folio numbers of his copy A—that is, the copy now in the *Overgekomen Brieven, Inkomend Briefboek Makassar* [*Letters Received, Inbound Letter Book Makassar*], 1671 KA 116, Folios 684–1007. We are grateful to Dr Noorduyn for a photocopy of relevant typescript pages.

35 Folio 726A.

36 Folios 726A to 729A.

Speelman glosses over the drama of the reign of La Icca' with the bland statement that he was slain by his relatives since his reign brought no joy.[37] Speelman then justifies the succession of La Pattawe' by the new ruler's marriage, supposedly to a sister of La Icca', rather than by the descent of La Pattawe' from Makkalempié, and his interest in replacing the man who had killed his father. Here, as in several other places, Speelman's account of Bone's affairs seems to reflect information derived from sources primarily concerned with Gowa. It remains, of course, extremely valuable for any comprehensive history of the period it covers, but it can be passed over in the attempt to understand more about the chronicle.

The political and cultural circumstances within which Speelman's successors managed the affairs of the Dutch East India Company in South Sulawesi usually gave little opportunity or incentive for gathering specific detail on the earlier history of the several kingdoms. The position of observers not associated with the company was even less favourable. Thus, for Nicolas Gervaise, writing at the end of the seventeenth century but whose testimony is rather questionable, the events of the 1660s are already legendary and there is little mention of kingdoms other than Gowa. The single sentence devoted to Bone does no more than confirm Bone's contemporary importance (Gervaise 1701: 60).[38] A good index of the lack of European knowledge on the period before the seventeenth century is its almost complete absence from François Valentijn's great compilation of data about Sulawesi—and much else—in the early eighteenth century. His account, which is very detailed, if somewhat unreliable, of matters that can be derived from Dutch sources has little more than a few guesses on matters earlier than 1600 (Valentijn 1858: Vol. 3, p. 120).

By far the most important eighteenth-century discussion of Bone's early history is to be found in Roelof Blok's *History of the Island of Celebes*, completed, but not published, in 1759.[39] In his preface, Blok criticises the errors in Valentijn's account of 'native Maccassar affairs' and, recalling

37 Folio 726B.

38 The original French edition, published in 1688, seems to be based on information from two Makasar nobles he met in Thailand and accompanied back to France. There is no evidence Gervaise himself visited Sulawesi.

39 Blok was the Dutch East India Company's governor and director in Makassar from 1756 to 1760. The preface to the work is dated 31 December 1759. The original work, or a copy, seems to have been retained in Fort Rotterdam and was accessible to J. von Stebenvoll, who, during the English period, made an English translation; this was published as Blok (1817). A Dutch version was published in *Tijdschrift voor Nederlandsch Indië*, Vol. 10, 1848, pp. 3–77.

Speelman's admission of some lost notes, implies he has access to 'the manuscripts of the Boneers and Maccassars'. Even more explicitly, he asserts

> that the ancient Histories of these countries are found among very few people, and that of Bone with the present King only, who has often declared to me his intention to burn them, if ever the Boneers should dethrone him (which may very easily happen,) for he should then consider his posterity unworthy of being acquainted with the origin of their ancestors …
>
> The writer, in compiling this [account], has followed the manuscripts of Bone, and of the Maccassars, respecting the more ancient events, and the notes of Mr. Speelman, in regard to the intermediate History, in such a manner, that, where some contradictions appeared, he selected the most probable account.
>
> Concerning the latter times, he has used the above mentioned manuscripts, and the journals, and memoirs of the successive Governors, lodged in the Secretary's office, and also such credible information, as he obtained from some aged native Kings and Princes. (Blok 1817: Vol. 1, pp. i–ii)

There can be no doubt Blok had access to some Bugis material on the history of Bone and, as the head of the Dutch East India Company's affairs in Makassar, was in a good position to have them translated. He begins his account with the first ruler, Matasilompo'é, and the general outline of his narrative is easily matched with the chronicle. Yet it is easy to find details in Blok's material that cannot be drawn from the chronicle in the form we have it or even that contradict statements in the chronicle. For a simple example, Blok supplies the names of all five children of the first ArumPone, where the chronicle is very explicit in giving only two (Blok 1817: Vol. 1, p. 36). A more interesting case concerns the death of Boté'é, the sixth ArumPone, who was slain by his brother's son. Blok adds a note: 'This is according to the notes of Speelman; but the manuscripts of Bone mention nothing of it' (Blok 1817: Vol. 1, p. 38).[40] Yet the chronicle, in its account of the murder of Boté'é, is quite explicit that this is what happened, thus suggesting Blok did not have access to the chronicle. It would be hard, however, to prove conclusively from these and other examples that Blok had not seen the chronicle as we have it, for he notes himself 'some contradictions' from which he 'selected the

40 This is as stated in Speelman's *Notitie*, Folio 726A.

most probable account' and he may well have had a source rather like the chronicle. His general outline of events is accurate. He is also perceptive: when asserting the early importance of Luwu, he notes 'this both the Boneers and Maccassars deny, though the fabulous History of the Boneers themselves make[s] it very clear' (Blok 1817: Vol. 1, p. 3).

Blok's account was not immediately available to everyone and the English captain Thomas Forrest, who was not allowed to land in Makassar in 1763, knew nothing of it (Forrest 1792: 72–3). The Dutch Rear Admiral J.S. Stavorinus, however, on his visit to Makassar in 1775, was sufficiently senior and inquisitive to have 'the perusal' of a translation of the Gowa chronicle and Blok's manuscript fell 'into my hands'. His slight information on early Bone is credited to Blok (Stavorinus 1798: Vol. 2, pp. 191, 193, 214–15).

The attention of the British scholars at the beginning of the nineteenth century was primarily focused on the history of the western parts of the archipelago, though the British period in Makassar did result in the translation of Blok's manuscript. Other information about early Bone appears in the oral account delivered to Raffles by 'the Bugis ambassador' in 1814.[41] After a short introduction, possibly drawn from some La Galigo material, the ambassador gave a remarkably full account of the *tomanurung* story and the reign of the first ArumPone, Matasilompo'é. This certainly shows a familiarity with material very like the first sections of the chronicle. The lack of further information is probably due to the circumstances of the visit and the need for someone to translate and transcribe. It is not clear what language the ambassador was speaking, but it was probably Malay (Raffles 1817: Vol. 2, pp. clxxix–xxxi).

As noted above, John Crawfurd had a Malay translation of the chronicle and possibly a copy of the Bugis text obtained on his visit to Makassar in 1814 (Crawfurd 1820: Vol. 2, p. 390n.). He also had material from Gowa and in some cases it is difficult to decide whether particular items of information come from the Gowa or the Bone chronicles or from another source altogether. For example, when dealing with the spread of Islam from Gowa, Crawfurd describes the approach of the ruler of Gowa to the ArumPone, offering 'to consider him in all respects as his equal' if

41 Cense (1966: 426–7) quotes extensively from a Bugis diary that describes a visit to see Raffles in Bogor over several days in May 1814. A microfilm of the diary may be found in the Cense papers, Or. 545, item 269 in the Leiden University Library. Though the diarist does not mention giving this oral account of early Bone, this is the most likely occasion on which it could have occurred.

only he would convert (Crawfurd 1820: Vol. 2, p. 385). This sounds like an abbreviated version of material in the Bone chronicle in the reign of La Tenrirua, Matinroé riBantaéng. On the other hand, the account of La Maddaremmeng aggressively trying to spread his religious ideas to other states, which then appealed to Gowa for protection, is in neither relevant chronicle (Crawfurd 1820: Vol. 2, p. 386). The most interesting aspect of Crawfurd's work in relation to early South Sulawesi is his attempt to assign dates to early reigns by counting back average reign lengths from a known point (Crawfurd 1820: Vol. 2, pp. 380–1). Though the arithmetic is not clear, this leads him to date the accession of La Ummasa', the second ArumPone, to 1366 CE. He then grants the following ruler, La Saliwu, a reign from 1398 to 1470, or 72 years, as stated in the Bone chronicle. Crawfurd also knows that La Saliwu's daughter, Wé Benrigau', Daéng Maroa, succeeded him and her son, La Tenrisukki', succeeded in turn, allegedly in 1490 (Crawfurd 1820: Vol. 2, pp. 485–7). All these names and relationships are given for the relevant early rulers in the Bone chronicle and it is difficult to see where else Crawfurd could have found them.

Another account of Bone's early history is found in the second part of a general history of Sulawesi, probably put together by W.R. van Hoëvell and published by him in 1854. This includes a well-informed summary of the material covered in the Bone chronicle, though there is no indication of the source of the information (van Hoëvell 1854: 213–15).

10. Previous editions and published translations of the chronicle

Strictly speaking, the first printed version of the chronicle is to be found in the first volume of B.F. Matthes's *Boegineesche Chrestomathie* published in Makassar in 1864 (Matthes 1864: 465–501). The whole work, as understood here, is followed by a list of ArumPone up to 1860. As noted above, this is all in Bugis characters and probably had few readers, especially non-Bugis readers, before the notes appeared in the third volume of the work, published in Amsterdam in 1872 (Matthes 1872: 60–78). Matthes explains in the introduction to his notes that the text is based on what became NBG 99, and the relevant pages of that manuscript are heavily annotated by Matthes. It seems likely the manuscript itself was used by the printer, though with some minor emendations by Matthes based on the manuscripts that became NBG 100 and NBG 101.

The first direct translation of a major part of the work appeared at much the same time, in a long article by Johannes Anthonius Bakkers. A friend of Matthes's, with whom he shared various journeys in South Sulawesi, Bakkers initially had a military career. In 1849, at age 40, he transferred into civil administration and spent the next 27 years closely involved with the affairs of the area. He served as governor of Celebes and dependencies from 1865 to his death in 1876. He was attached, effectively as the political officer, to both the 1859 and 1860 Dutch expeditions against Bone and it is tempting to believe he was present when the ArumPone's house at Pasémpe' was looted on 9 December 1859. He also spent time in Bone after the war. On 10 December 1863, he completed an extensive account of all he had discovered about Bone (Bakkers 1866). This contains two items of interest. The first is a detailed genealogy of Bone's rulers and their families from Matasilompo'é to the 27th ArumPone, Bessé Kajuara, who fled from Pasémpe' (Bakkers 1866: 154–68). The second is a translation of roughly half the chronicle—that is, to a point about halfway through the account of the reign of Bongkangngé, Matinroé riGucinna, and based explicitly on the looted manuscript, now NBG 101 (Bakkers 1866: 169–83). The translation was probably done by Bakkers's regular translator, J. Bensbach, and Bakkers admits that Matthes might have done a better job (Bakkers 1866: 9, 169).[42] In fact, it does follow the text fairly closely. Bakkers also adds to both genealogy and chronicle references to Crawfurd's dates and he is aware of the imminent publication of the first volume of the *Boegineesche Chrestomathie*. Given the friendship between Matthes and Bakkers, it is easy to understand how the manuscript had been made available to Matthes while preparing the text of his volume and how it ended up in Matthes's collection as NBG 101.

Although Matthes suggests translations of various difficult passages in his notes to the text, his only treatment of a longer passage from the chronicle is a close paraphrase of the *tomanurung* section in a collection of Bugis and Makasar legends (Matthes 1885: 6–7). The same section has

42 It is a suspicious coincidence that Matthes's detailed annotations to the manuscript cease only a page and a half after the point at which Bakkers's translation ends.

been very carefully translated, explicitly based on the text in *Boegineesche Chrestomathie*, by Kern (1929: 307–10), alongside similar passages relating to Soppeng, Tanete and Luwu.

In 1981, the text of the whole chronicle, transliterated into Latin characters and provided with an Indonesian translation, was published in Jakarta as one element in an anthology of Bugis historical texts (Chairan et al. 1981). Four of the items, including the Bone chronicle, are credited to Tamin Chairan. Most of the volume—perhaps all of it—is drawn directly from *Boegineesche Chrestomathie*. The system of transliteration differs somewhat from that used here, but it is carefully done, and the translation is clear and effective.

A similar, but less careful, volume appeared in 1992–93 (Hamid and Kartikasari 1992–93). The manuscript on which the text is based is not stated and the transliteration is rather careless. The translation is much more stilted than in the previous volume.

Finally, a much longer version of the chronicle, in Lontara' characters, has recently been published (Muhlis et al. 2018). This brings the narrative up to the middle of the twentieth century. For the earlier parts of this version, reference is made to other manuscripts of the work as understood here. The editors suggest the archetype of much of the later text may have been written in the nineteenth century, with sections later than that written after Indonesian independence (Muhlis et al. 2018: xxv–vi).[43]

11. Commentary on the chronicle

While the chronicle is a major source for the early history of Bone, any full historical account would need to consider other Bugis and Makasar works, as well as the results of archaeological investigations and other relevant information. This is not the place for such a task. The following commentary draws attention to various historical and cultural aspects of the chronicle and is intended to help those wishing to make use of the work for their own purposes.

43 For the sake of completeness, we also mention an unpublished typescript Indonesian translation of the *Boegineesche Chrestomathie* text made available to us by the late Christian Pelras.

Chapter 1

The chronicle opens with a statement of its subject: '[T]he land of Bone and the ruling of Bone.' The Bugis wording is a standard expression for the contents of a section of manuscript, so that this first sentence amounts to a title for the work. Before the chronicle proper begins, however, there is an elaborate statement of exculpation, excusing the author from the consequences of naming high-status individuals. This exculpation is continued in the frequent occurrence throughout the chronicle of the expression 'may my belly not swell' before the first mention of an ArumPone's personal name.[44] The personal names usually begin with *La* for males and *Wé* for females, while *I* can be used for either. This mark of respect for a name that represents the person himself or herself relates directly to the all-pervasive status system in the society, and similar restrictions are found in many cultures. To avoid the problem of repeated use of personal names, other elements in the naming system are used. The most common in the chronicle is the necronym or name applied at the time of death and usually associated with some aspect of that death—for example, the eleventh ArumPone is known as Matinroé riBantaéng or 'He who sleeps at Bantaeng' because he died and was buried there, where his grave is still preserved. He also held, at least at the outset of his reign, the independent posts as Arung or king of Palakka and of Pattiro. Another less frequent naming strategy, at least for the very highest level, is the teknonym or naming a man after his child; the twelfth ArumPone was thus named To Akkempéang. Several ArumPone have nicknames that are used freely; thus, the name Kerrampélua', for the third ArumPone, derives from the fact his hair stood up immediately after his birth. The introductory section ends with a statement about the structure of the chronicle, which is to follow the genealogical line of the rulers.

The chronicle then addresses the issue of ultimate origins; if its structure depends on the succession of rulers, what came before the succession began in Bone? There is brief reference to the succession of rulers in the La Galigo cycle of stories that holds such a prominent place in Bugis culture.[45] Concepts of kingship and status lie at the heart of this

44 Cummings (2007: 51) notes that some versions of the Gowa chronicle begin with very similar passages and a parallel expression of exculpation occurs throughout both the Gowa and the Tallo chronicles.

45 The similar reference to the La Galigo cycle in the Soppeng chronicle (Caldwell 1988: 109) is probably inspired by the Bone chronicle. Stephen Druce points out in a personal communication that such references are not found in texts from the western coast of the peninsula.

'tribal encyclopaedia', but this is a world that is generally admitted to have gone.[46] For the purposes of a chronicle, setting things out in order, the obvious place for the La Galigo stories is before the real story begins. This then leaves a chronological space, here reckoned at seven generations, for a period of chaos. The descriptive elements applied to this period have the ring of set tropes; they refer to the lack of settled arrangements, whether formally constituted or mere custom, and especially in relation to agreed and acknowledged status. The reference to fish eating one another goes back to Indic sources (Basham 1971: 87).

The beginning of the sequence of kings is explicitly announced and the chronicle launches into an elaborate *tomanurung* story. These stories are found across South Sulawesi and, as noted above, serve to explain, or least justify, the system of ascribed status. The significance of the events about to unfold is marked by a week of lightning, thunder and an earthquake strongly reminiscent of the signs around the birth of Hayam Wuruk as recorded in the *Deśawarṇana*.[47] Thunder and lightning also mark the disappearance of the first ruler and his consort.

The role of the 'people' in seeking a social contract with the *tomanurung*, and then agreeing to one, has been much commented on (Henley and Caldwell 2008), and this agreement is explicitly passed down the line of succession.

The name Bone is used here—and very often later in the chronicle—in a geographical sense. A royal hall was set up here for the *tomanurung*. This was in the centre of the modern town of Watampone, which means the 'capital of Bone'. Etymologically, the name, which is found in various forms throughout the peninsula, seems to refer to the sandy nature of the site. The scale of events at this early stage is limited to Matajang, just outside the centre of Bone, and Toro', a few kilometres to the east. No other rulers are mentioned beyond the immediate family of the first ArumPone. The work of the ruler is seen in his role in establishing legal arrangements, especially for trade, and in the possession of a war banner.

---

46 There were some attempts in Luwu to link La Galigo rulers with the historical series, but these seem to be late rationalisations. For further discussion of the cultural significance and affiliations of the La Galigo cycle, see Macknight (2003).

47 *Deśawarṇana*, 4.3, 4 in Robson (1995: 26).

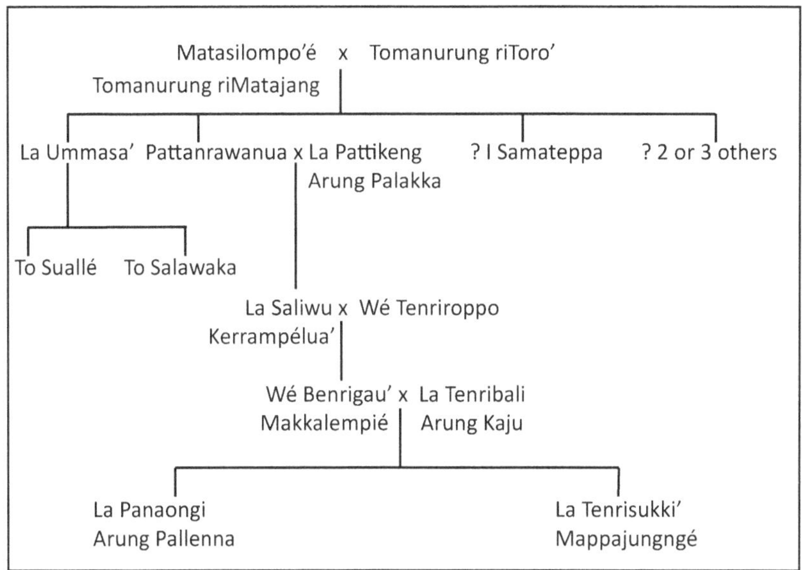

Figure 1 The genealogy of the early rulers

Chapter 2

With the accession of La Ummasa', the second ArumPone, the chronicle takes on a strongly 'realist' style, as discussed above. The necronym of 'Our lord who first had a grave' indicates the chronicle is now moving beyond legend and into an account of the deeds of real people who die and need to be buried. The geographical range of interest is extended to other nearby settlements through conquest and marriage.

The major part of the chapter is given over to the story of snatching the ArumPone's infant nephew from Palakka and installing him as the succeeding ArumPone. The need for this dramatic intervention is spelt out explicitly: since the two sons of La Ummasa' lacked sufficient status because of their low-status mother, they could not succeed, but the sister of La Ummasa', who shared his status, brought that to her marriage with the king of Palakka, whom it is assumed derived his status by descent from another *tomanurung*, so their child does inherit appropriate status from both parents. This is a very clear demonstration of the mutual recognition of status between polities. The ceremony associated with the baby's umbilical cord and afterbirth in Bone marks his identification with Bone, rather than Palakka. The reality of the baby's authority is emphasised by the need for La Ummasa' to seek permission for something as unexceptional as travel.

Chapter 3

The account of the long reign of Kerrampélua' opens with a recapitulation of the story of his installation as a baby. It should be noted that the name most used for this king, Kerrampélua', or 'Standing hair', refers to his appearance when born; the use of the name itself is a reminder of these events. The realism of the story is then confirmed and extended by a description of the practical arrangements by which the rule of the baby was organised. The care with which these matters are set out strongly suggests the author of the chronicle in the seventeenth century felt the need to explain the obvious problem of a baby exercising the responsibilities of rule. This concern for a seventeenth-century audience confirms the essential unity of the chronicle as a work in the mind of its creator.

During this reign, Bone established its supremacy across the coastal plain and into the neighbouring hills.

Although described in terms of placenames, the listing of the military forces makes it clear that the essential element was the control of people, rather than of territory. The same point can be seen when Makkalempié, the daughter of Kerrampélua', is set up as the ruler of Majang, one of the places conquered by her great uncle La Ummasa'. It was necessary to move people from Bukaka, close to Bone in the north, to Majang, about 4 kilometres southwest, presumably to offer support to Makkalempié. The process of expansion was not straightforward and Anrobiring, which was another of the places conquered by La Ummasa', had to be reconquered. Three lists of conquests are given and, since the names fall into groups progressively further out across the plain, they may represent distinct campaigns. Even further away, there were rulers who were happy to merge their lands with Bone and, in the important case of Kaju, this was confirmed by the marriage of its ruler with Makkalempié.

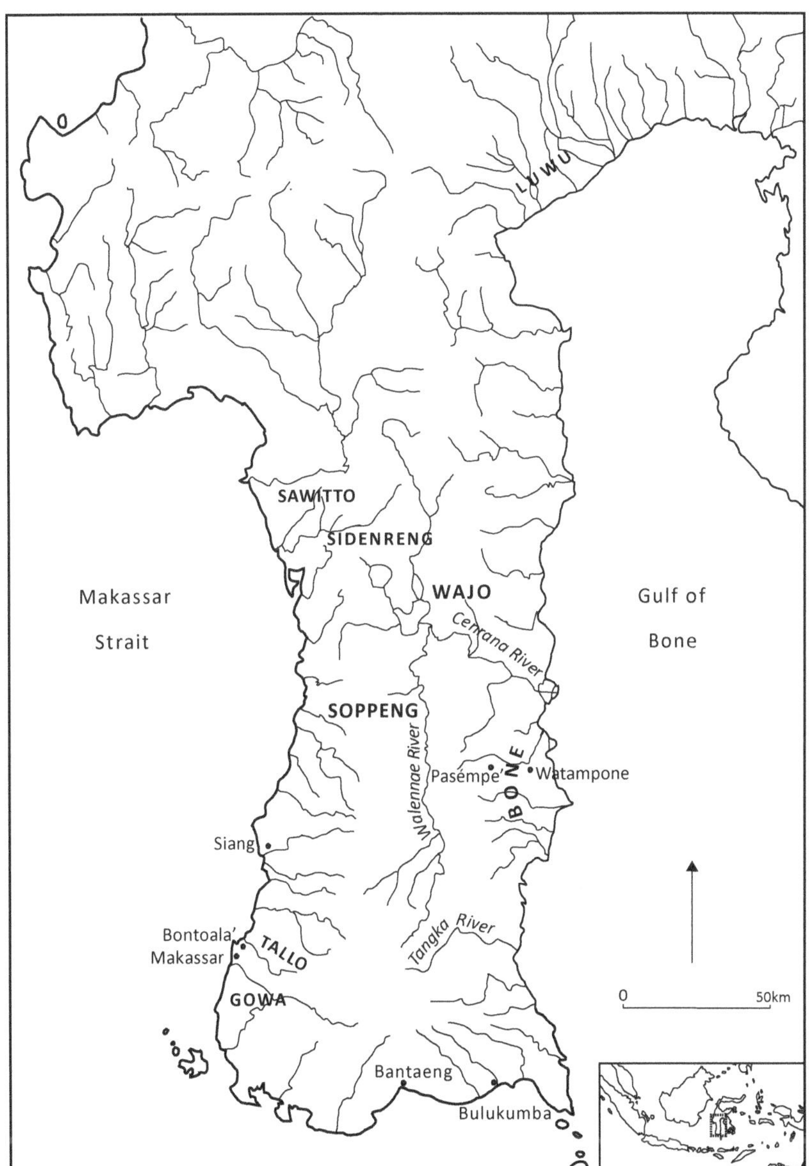

Map 1 South Sulawesi

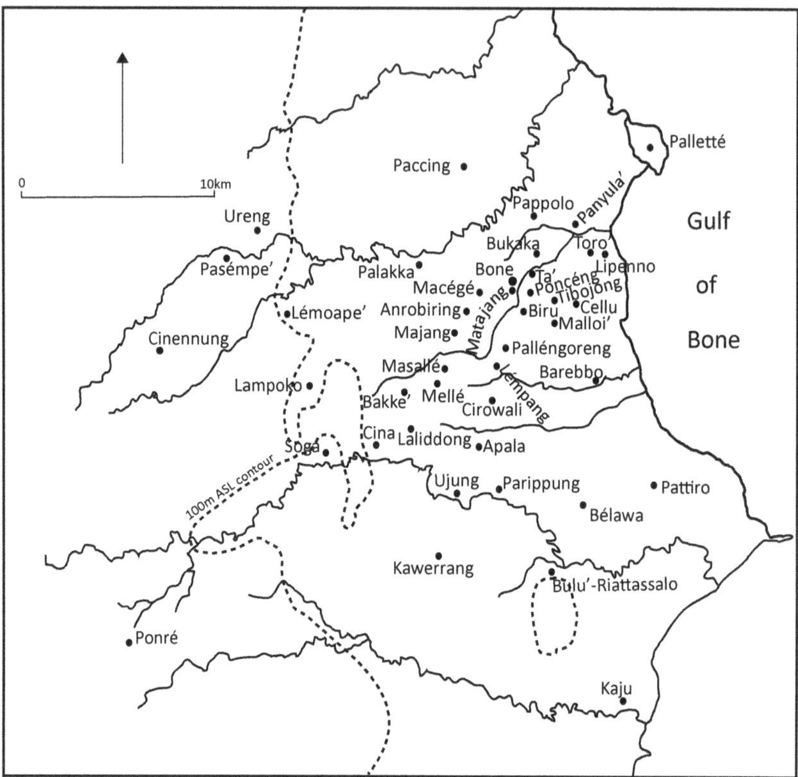

Map 2 The early expansion of Bone

Macknight (1983) has argued that this record of conquests reveals an expansion of wet rice cultivation through increased control of water sources. This was supported by military and political successes leading to a multiplier effect by which various elements of development lend each other mutual reinforcement. The reference to Kerrampélua' initiating a system of cursing enemies might relate to some innovations in ceremony and the supernatural belief system that would also provide another element in change.

Another aspect of the economy is mentioned with the settlement of people to the north-east at Panyula', about 4 kilometres downstream on the minor river that flows near Bone. These slaves, who belonged to Kerrampélua' himself, along with those also settled at the settlement of Lipenno, supplied fish and provided personal services as paddlers bearers.

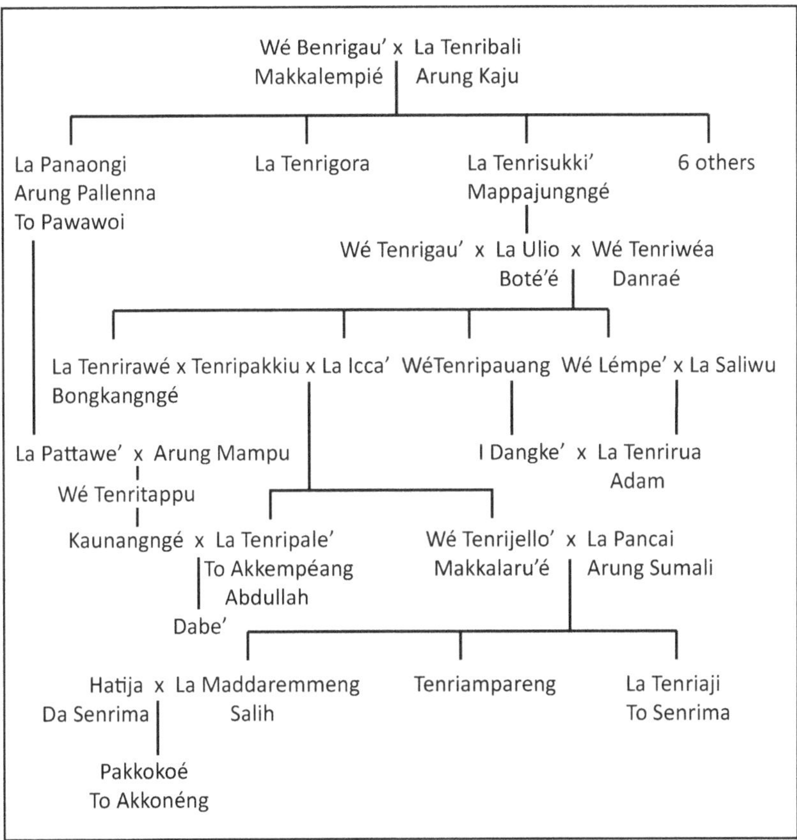

Figure 2 The descendants of Wé Benrigau', Makkalempié

Note: This lists those who became ArumPone with their number in the sequence of chapters distinguished in the chronicle. It also provides a more complete account of the names and titles of each individual. The genealogical information in the figure is by no means complete and has been selected to illustrate the main points made in the chronicle in relation to succession as ArumPone.

4. Wé Benrigau', Makkalempié, Daéng Maroa, Bissu reLalempili', Arung Majang, Puatta riLawélareng, Mallajangngé riCina

5. La Tenrisukki', Mappajungngé

6. La Ulio, Boté'é, Matinroé rItterrung

7. La Tenrirawé, Bongkangngé, Matinroé riGucinna

8. La Icca', Matinroé riAddénénna

9. La Pattawe', Arung Kaju, Matinroé riBettung

10. Wé Tenritappu, Matinroé riSidénréng

11. La Tenrirua, Arung Palakka, Arung Pattiro, Adam, Matinroé riBantaéng

12. La Tenripale', To Akkempéang, Arung Timurung, Abdullah, Matinroé riTallo'

13. La Maddaremmeng, Arung Timurung, Salih, Matinroé riBukaka

La Tenriaji, To Senrima, Arung AwamPoné, Pawélaié riSiang

La Tenritatta, To Unru', Arung Palakka, Datu Mario-Riwawo, Daéng Sérang, Sa'aduddin, Petta Malampé'é Gemme'na, Matinroé riBontoala'

Chapter 4

The only child of Kerrampélua' mentioned in the previous chapter was a daughter, Makkalempié, and she succeeded to the position of ArumPone following the explicit wish of her parents. The fact she was a woman occasions no special comment. As a girl, she had previously been installed as the ruler of Majang, as noted above, and married the ruler of Kaju, further south. As in the account of the first ArumPone, only two of the nine children of the marriage are named and they both have a later role in the narrative.

Most of the account of the reign is taken up with agricultural expansion, both by purchase and by conquest, in and around Cina and Laliddong at the base of the hills about 10 kilometres southwest of Bone. This area, which lies beyond Majang, clearly had some special attraction for Makkalempié as one of her sons was given control of both Cina and Majang and she herself abdicated and retired to Cina.

The author of the chronicle, who is now well into a 'realistic' style, seems at a loss to know what to make of the story of Makkalempié's death. Her necronym, 'She who disappeared in Cina', could not be avoided and needed some explanation, which the story provides, but the account of some sort of ball lightning removing her from the house sounds legendary.

Chapter 5

La Tenrisukki' inherited the role of ArumPone from his mother, Makkalempié, at a young age, though the figure of only 11 years found in this version of the chronicle is hard to believe and perhaps the 19 years found elsewhere is more credible, especially given a younger brother had already established himself in Cina at the time of their mother's abdication. Marrying his first cousin at least four years after the abdication does not decide the matter one way or another. Such a marriage was entirely proper, indeed perhaps preferable, in high-status Bugis society since it ensured the status of any resulting children.

La Tenrisukki' acquired his nickname, Mappajungngé, 'He who uses an umbrella', through the capture of the invading Luwu ruler's *pajung* or umbrella—a mark of high status. Again, we see in this and in the injunction not to harm the person of the Datu of Luwu the mutual respect of rulers. No reason is given for the invasion of Bone's territory by the army of Luwu. It may have been a deliberate attempt by Luwu to reassert earlier dominance in the central area of the peninsula; or it may simply have been a raiding party from the sea, possibly directed towards the capture of women rather than territory. The battle was fought out across the settlements 3 or 4 kilometres south of Bone that had been captured by the second ArumPone, La Ummasa'. The site of Cellu where the Luwu forces established themselves is about 2 kilometres inland, while the Bone base at Biru is another 3 kilometres further west. It is difficult to follow the fighting that transpired since the exact location of Attassalo is not known, but the rout of the forces of Luwu was decisive and the Datu was lucky to escape by sea with a handful of supporters.

The war with Mampu in the north looks like a more straightforward competition for territory. Its resolution, however, is cast in terms of incorporating the ruler, his family and his following into the status system of Bone. The possibility of plunder is explicitly rejected.

Both these conflicts show Bone beginning to deal with other significant polities to the north. The range of interaction has been considerably extended beyond that of earlier reigns.

Chapter 6

The succession of the Mappajungngé's son, La Ulio, Boté'é or the 'Fat man', was straightforward. After various personal qualities are mentioned, his marriage to the daughter of the ruler of Pattiro, nearly 20 kilometres down the coast to the south, is mentioned. Each of the four of the children whose names are recorded went on to play a significant role in later chapters.

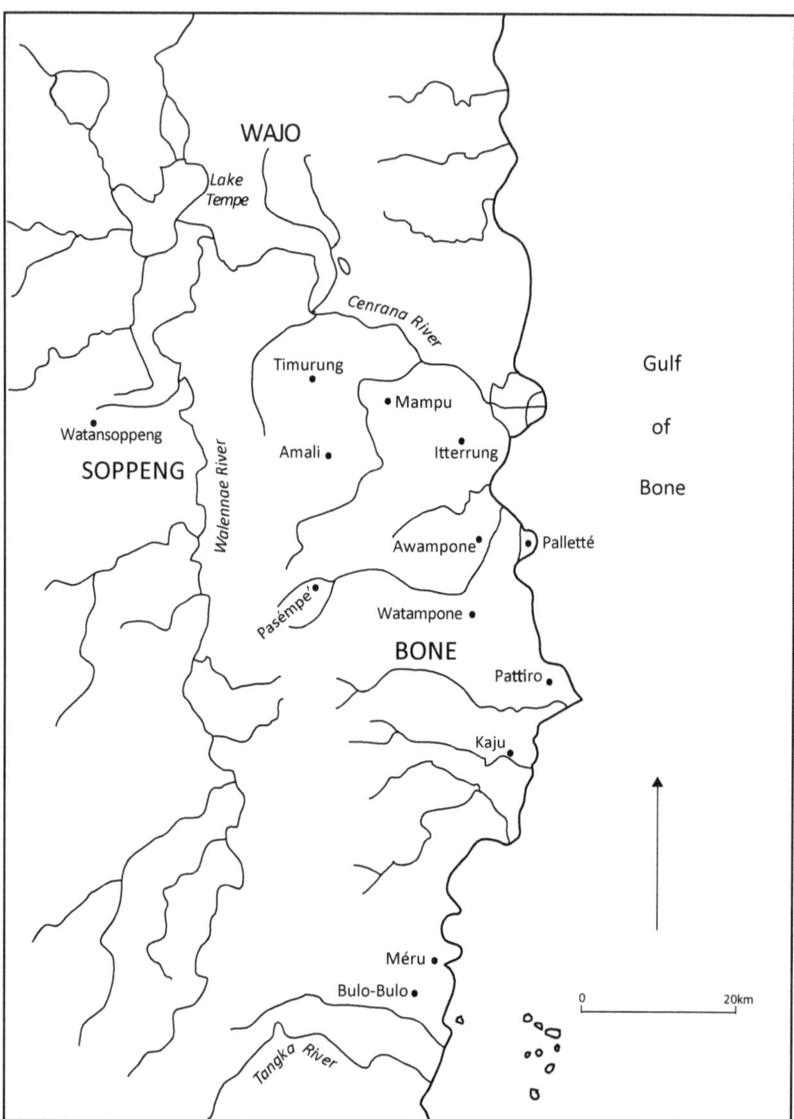

Map 3 Bone and its immediate neighbours

The reign of Boté'é marks a further dramatic expansion in the field of war and politics, as well as growing sophistication in administration. Thus, a central figure in the customary law texts of later times, Kajao Laliddong or the Sage of Laliddong, is assigned to this reign. More immediately, the reign sees the beginning of the long and complex relationship with the Makasar state of Gowa.[48] This began well enough with a treaty between Boté'é and Tumapa'risi' Kallonna, the Karaeng or ruler of Gowa, which was duly noted in the chronicle of Gowa (Cummings 2007: 32).[49] There was further conflict with Luwu and the alliance with Gowa was confirmed when the new ruler, Tunipalangga, succeeded his father. After a meeting between rulers on the Cenrana River in the north—perhaps in the course of the campaign against Luwu—Tunipalangga came to Bone itself and a detailed treaty was agreed to, covering reciprocal legal rights. There was then a further joint victory against Wajo in the north.

This interest in the north was confirmed by the ArumPone's second marriage, with the daughter of the ruler of Mampu, an area that had been conquered in the previous reign. The integration of this new northern territory and its people seems to have been incomplete, however, and Boté'é tried to resolve issues by making a clear distinction between his northern following and his southern following. This involved installing his young son, by the southern mother, as ArumPone and allowing northerners to identify as followers of his wife from Mampu. In what amounted to a family row, Boté'é ended up being killed at Itterrung, which provided his necronym.

Chapter 7

La Tenrirawé, or Bongkangngé, had already been installed as ArumPone before his father's death. Perhaps to mend the division between north and south, he married a ruler from Timurung, well to the northwest, but neither of their children survived. After the usual list of personal matters, details are given of further administrative arrangements as well as a note on the introduction of guns.

Most of the long chapter, however, is given over to the struggle with Gowa, which had embarked on a policy of aggressive expansion. Contrasting views of events can be seen in the respective chronicles of the two sides. The opening episode reads almost as a cheeky story of a cockfighting

48 The other side of this relationship can be followed in the chronicles of Gowa and Tallo (Cumming 2007). Further information is supplied in the Wajo chronicle edited by Noorduyn and his introduction provides an excellent account of these interactions through the sixteenth century (Noorduyn 1955: 73–92).

49 Noorduyn (1955: 74) suggests this was signed in Gowa. The text of the treaty was published by Matthes (1864: 531–2).

victory by Bongkangngé, who had wagered his private possession of the people of Panyula', inherited from Kerrampélua', over his guest, presumably Tunipalangga, who lost a significant sum of money.

Before the struggle with Gowa began, Bone strengthened its position with an alliance 'west of the wood'—that is, in the north around Pampanua—and by further conquests or reconquests on the plain to the south. In the far south, three communities on the Tangka River—Bulo-Bulo, Lamatti and Raja—were made vassals of Bone.

Despite these defensive moves, the forces of Gowa invaded and there was a protracted battle south of Méru, which is very close to Bone itself. From the Gowa chronicle, we learn this was part of a widespread series of campaigns across South Sulawesi under Tunipalangga. Among many other places, the three communities on the Tangka River were conquered and it is noted specifically that only Bone was not conquered (Cummings 2007: 33–5). As the Bone chronicle records, in the peace treaty that concluded this episode, the southern boundary of Bone was agreed to be the Tangka River.

As a result of Gowa's aggression, various refugees arrived in Bone, including the ruler of Sawitto on the west coast[50] and the losing party in royal squabbles in Soppeng. The marriage of this Soppeng noble with the ArumPone's sister set up family ties between Soppeng and Bone. A more surprising refugee was Tunipalangga's nephew, known in the Gowa chronicle as Tunijallo' but in the Bone chronicle as Daéng Pabéta or, in a play on words, as Daéng Patobo'. This was the outcome of a romantic entanglement that caused offence, as detailed in the Gowa chronicle (Cummings 2007: 38).

The struggle continued with another attack by Gowa at Cellu, where Bone under Mappajungngé had fought off the forces of Luwu, but the usually victorious Tunipalangga was wounded and retreated. Two years later, he tried again, building a fort as a base. After a period of fighting, he became ill, retreated again and died.

Tunipalangga's brother, known in Bone as Daéng Parukka and in Gowa as Tunibatta, then took up the fight. After summoning his son, Tunijallo', to return to Gowa, he embarked on yet another campaign. This caused

50 Druce (2009: 83–4) has published an account of this from the perspective of Sawitto.

a degree of panic and desertion among Bone's allies and the forces of Gowa were able to build a fort at Pappolo only 3 kilometres or so north of Bone and destroy villages even closer in. In a final push, however, Tunibatta was driven back and killed.

In the face of this calamity, Gowa turned to the much respected ruler of Tallo, known to the Bugis as Daéng Padulung and to the Makasar as Tumenanga riMakkoayang. He and Kajao Laliddong, who served as adviser to both Bongkangngé and his father, Boté'é, sorted out the terms of a treaty; Tunijallo', who had after all fought with Bone against his uncle Tunipalangga, was allowed to succeed his father as Karaeng of Gowa and that presumably satisfied the victors.

There was then further conflict with Luwu in the north, with fighting at Cenrana on the river and the enslavement of people at Unyi, just south of the river. Whereas under Boté'é, Bone had been the enemy of Wajo, Gowa's recent aggression prompted a change and Wajo and Bone worked together against Luwu at Cenrana. This new alignment of powers was formalised in a grand alliance between Bone, Wajo and Soppeng. Soppeng, too, had been attacked by Gowa. This agreement, known as Tellumpoccoé or the 'Three Powers', was instituted at Timurung, a convenient central point, and was of enduring importance. It is convincingly dated to 1582 (Noorduyn 1955: 84).

Bongkangngé died two years later and, since he had no surviving children, he was succeeded by his brother, La Icca'. His death name, Matinroé riGucinna or 'He who sleeps in his urn', appears to be a reference to the pre-Islamic practice of interring the cremated remains of a notable person in a large Chinese jar.

Chapter 8

La Icca' inherited from his brother not only the kingdom, but also his wife, the ruler of Timurung, with whom he had three children. Of the two who survived, one, La Tenripale', became the twelfth ArumPone and the other, Wé Tenrijello', became the mother of the successor of La Tenripale'.

One final attack from Gowa ended inconclusively in the face of the joint Tellumpoccoé forces.[51]

51 The Gowa chronicle gives more detail on this but is difficult to interpret (Cummings 2007: 41).

In presenting an account of the dramatic events of the reign, the author of the chronicle admits to not knowing what La Icca' was thinking when he embarked on a series of unjustified murders and tyrannical decisions. The crisis came when a fire, lit by La Icca', spread throughout the settlement, causing widespread destruction. People fleeing the fire demanded something be done.

The places mentioned in the story provide an indication of the extent of settlement. The centre of Bone appears to have been more or less in the official area of modern Watampone and within the walls that were in place during the Dutch attack in 1859 (Perelaer 1872: Maps).[52] Matajang lies less than 1 kilometre to the south and Macégé' is about the same distance to the west—both well within the modern town. The statement that the fire spread up to and beyond these places, however, suggests that fairly dense settlement extended well beyond the wall. The mention later in the story of all the houses within the wall being burnt confirms the existence of a wall at that time, possibly enclosing much the same area as in the nineteenth century. Majang is only about 4 kilometres to the southwest of the centre so the fire could easily be seen from there. If Da Malaka, the critical conspirator, was already coming from Mampu in the north and skirting west of Bone, it makes sense that he came through Palakka, about 4 kilometres northwest of Bone.

The discussion between the lord of Majang and his nephew Da Malaka over the propriety of regicide is revealing. The essential point is that no one subsidiary ruler can override the status of a paramount ruler—in this case, the ArumPone—but, given just cause, an alliance of subsidiary rulers can be justified in usurping power and, in this case, killing the ArumPone. It is not clear why the lord of Majang took a leading role in the rebellion, but perhaps his advanced age gave him particular respect.

Chapter 9

The choice of La Pattawe' as the new ArumPone was determined by the lord of Majang, who had played such an important part in killing La Icca', the previous ArumPone, and it involved a major shift in the line of descent. A sufficient nobility was assured through the father of La Pattawe', who was a son of the fourth ruler, Makkalempié (Figure 2). The genealogy

52 In Chapter 13, La Maddaremmeng is recorded as extending the wall to the east and south.

in the hanging chart in Watampone, described in Appendix 2, also traces his descent through his mother to his great-grandmother, who was a sister of the third ruler, Kerrampélua'. His father, Arung Pallenna, was one of those killed by La Icca', which presumably assured his opposition to the previous regime.

It is difficult to know how old the new ArumPone was at his installation; given he was a whole generation closer to Makkalempié than his two predecessors, one could argue he must have been a mature man, at least, but against this is the statement that his grandfather, the lord of Majang, was still alive and active. The only noteworthy features of his seven-year reign were genealogical developments important for future reigns.

Chapter 10

The succession of the previous ArumPone's daughter, Wé Tenritappu, Matinroé riSidénréng, continued the alternative line of descent. Her institution of a council of seven leading nobles seems to have been designed partly to compensate for her being a woman, but it can equally be seen as a measure to bind the central parts of the wider kingdom more tightly together. It is worth noting that her claim to be descended from the fifth ArumPone, Mappajungngé, is through her mother, the daughter of Boté'é's second marriage with Wé Tenrigau' in Mampu.

This reign saw renewed conflict with Gowa, this time associated with the spread of Islam. This series of wars is also described in the Tallo chronicle (Cummings 2007) and dated in *The Makassar Annals* (Cummings 2010). In the first campaign, Gowa and its allies from Ajattappareng were defeated by the combined forces of Tellumpoccoé—that is, Bone, Wajo and Soppeng. This seems to have been in 1607 (Cummings 2010: 35). The following year, Gowa attacked again and defeated the Tellumpoccoé forces. A year later, this victory was followed up by attacking Soppeng alone, which was defeated and forcibly converted. The next year, 1610, the same fate befell Wajo, and the ArumPone, presumably sensing the way things were going, visited Sidénréng and personally converted. Her sudden death meant the question of a wider conversion in Bone was unresolved.

Chapter 11

The appointment of the new ArumPone, La Tenrirua, Matinroé riBantaéng, represented a return to the previous line of descent in several ways. His mother, I Lémpe', was the sister of Bongkangngé and La Icca' and her husband and the new ArumPone's father, La Saliwu, was her second cousin—that is, he too was descended from Mappajungngé.[53] La Tenrirua's marriage to Dangke', the daughter of Wé Tenripauang, a sister of his mother, had already been noted in Chapter 9.

La Tenrirua reigned for less than a year in 1611. The events of this reign and the next, which led to the formal Islamisation of Bone, are exceptional in the history of the spread of Islam. The story begins with another attack by the forces of Gowa, apparently under the control of Sultan Ala'uddin himself, who built two forts, one to the south at Cellu, which had so often been the site of conflict with invading forces, and the other at Pallette, an easily defended coastal outcrop to the north. Gowa's intention was clearly conversion. La Tenrirua attempted to persuade his people to accept Islam both because that would represent a benefit in itself and because alliance with Gowa, rather than defiance, would be in Bone's long-term interest. He was unsuccessful and withdrew to Pattiro, a promontory to the south that he held separately to his position in Bone, but he had no more success there in urging conversion. He was left with only his immediate family and courtiers.

The people of Bone then sent an envoy to remonstrate with him. The exchange of views, which has a sense of authenticity, is remarkable and illuminates the nature of kingship in Bone. To Alaung, the envoy, accuses La Tenrirua of deserting his loyal followers: 'It is not that we do not want you, but you do not want us.' As spelt out for the very first ArumPone, the *tomanurung*, rule involves a contract between ruler and ruled. In more prosaic terms, it is a patron–client relationship writ large.[54] In reply, La Tenrirua appealed to his desire to lead his people to a better future as Muslims. Faced with this impasse, the people of Bone turned to La Tenrirua's first cousin, the son of La Icca' and thus in the same line of descent. The new ArumPone, La Tenripale', Matinroé riTallo', continued to defy Gowa.

53 In fact, as the Bone family tree shows, La Tenrirua was the great-grandson, not grandson, of Mappajungngé, through both his father and his mother. See also Figure 2.

54 Pelras (2000) explores the patron–client relationship in modern South Sulawesi society.

The narrative then shifts to the personal relationship between the ruler of Gowa, Sultan Ala'uddin, and the deposed ArumPone, La Tenrirua. A force was sent to relieve Pattiro, rescue La Tenrirua and bring him to Palletté. There he was received courteously and his continued ownership of various territories, or rather the people living in them, was acknowledged. Both sides agreed on the importance of conversion and Sultan Ala'uddin, who claimed Palletté by right of conquest, gave it to La Tenrirua as a token of goodwill. When Sultan Ala'uddin tried to follow this up with an expensive personal gift, La Tenrirua initially refused it as a bribe, but was then persuaded that it was an appropriate gift between families.[55]

The terms in which the leaders then express their support for each other are remarkably personal and refer to their families and descendants. The presence of the ruler of Tallo at the time of the agreement is particularly significant. This was Karaeng Matoaya, Sultan Abdullah, who had acted as chief advisor to Sultan Ala'uddin since his accession, and the details of this campaign, along with many others in the wars of Islamisation, are given in the Tallo chronicle dealing with his reign. They are explicitly omitted from the Gowa chronicle (Cummings 2007: 44, 88).

Bone could not then hold out against the forces of Gowa and was defeated militarily, leading to the nominal conversion of the people of Bone by force and the reinstatement of La Tenrirua as ArumPone. This reinstatement could not last, however, and as soon as the forces of Gowa withdrew, La Tenrirua was driven out and fled to protection in Makassar. There he was instructed in Islam by Dato' riBandang—the teacher who had converted Sultan Ala'uddin six years earlier (Cummings 2007: 43)—and provided with the entirely suitable Muslim name of Adam. He then lived in retirement in Bantaeng on the south coast, where he died in 1631 (Cummings 2010: 42).

55 There is a significant problem with the chronicle's account of this. As it reads, the ruler of Gowa claims to be in a *besan* relationship with La Tenrirua—that is, a relationship of mutual in-laws. In fact, as set out in the following chapter and confirmed in the Gowa chronicle (Cummings 2007: 46), it was the next ArumPone, La Tenripale', and La Tenrirua's first cousin, whose daughter, Dabe', was promised to Daeng Mattola, or Sultan Malikussaid, the son of the ruler with whom La Tenrirua was dealing. All sources agree that Dabe' died in childhood. There is no easy solution to the problem. Was Sultan Ala'uddin using the *besan* link very loosely, perhaps thinking of Bone and Gowa as equivalent to families? Was La Tenripale' also at the meeting and did he, rather than La Tenrirua, receive the offer of the jacket, which seems unlikely given his continuing opposition to Gowa's demands?

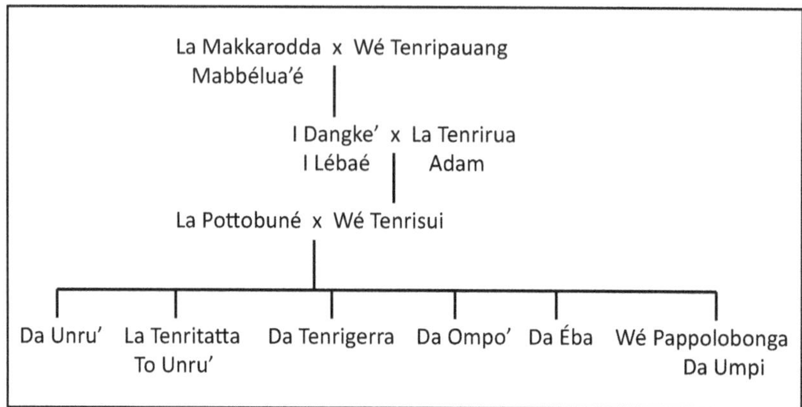

Figure 3 The descent and siblings of La Tenritatta, Arung Palakka, as described in the chronicle

Note: For the descent of La Tenrirua, Adam, see Figure 2.

Chapter 12

The name and descent of La Tenrirua's successor, La Tenripale', Matinroé riTallo', had already been introduced in the previous chapter in the account of his temporary role as ArumPone. With the final departure of La Tenrirua, his first cousin, La Tenripale' was the obvious successor. After one final attempt to throw off the Makasar oppressor and escape conversion, the people of Bone and their vassals succumbed amid considerable destruction and accepted their new status as vassals of Gowa and as Muslims. La Tenripale' had no choice but to convert. The magnanimous terms imposed by the victors are credited in the Tallo chronicle to Karaeng Matoaya as a deliberate political move (Cummings 2007: 88) and they may have helped bring an end to the wars of Islamisation.

The genealogical details that follow trace out two lines of descent. The first runs through Wé Tenrijello', the younger sister of the ArumPone. Her eldest son was La Maddaremmeng, who was to succeed his uncle as ArumPone. Another son was La Tenriaji or To Senrima, who would also play an important role in the future. This line obtained two of the three minor kingdoms formerly held by La Tenrirua: Wé Tenrijello received Pattiro and La Tenriaji, AwamPoné. Family power was also affirmed by a third son becoming king in Cellu—the key defensive position near Bone.

The other line of descent goes back to La Tenrirua. His daughter, Wé Tenrisui, was the mother, most importantly, of La Tenritatta, Arung Palakka, but the full list of his siblings is given. The distinction between these two lines would be critical in the future.

The attachment of La Tenripale' to Islam and to the accommodation with Gowa and Tallo appears to have been genuine. He, too, was instructed in religion by Dato' riBandang and received a Muslim name. He also promised in marriage his only child to the son of the Gowa ruler, though she died young and no further marriage link was possible.[56] Towards the end of his life, he spent time in Makassar and *The Makassar Annals* records his death on 13 August 1630 (Cummings 2010: 41). Given his reign began in 1611, this fits with a total reign of 20 years as stated.

Chapter 13

The next ArumPone, La Maddaremmeng, Matinroé riBukaka, succeeded his uncle, but as explained in Section 8, the account of his reign is highly defective. It begins in the normal way with his names, marriage, son and a few details of the reign. The mention of his creation of a white umbrella—presumably in differentiation from the previous yellow umbrella—might be related to his enthusiasm for Islam. His extensions of the wall to the east and south probably brought it to about the same position as what the Dutch faced in 1859 (Perelaer 1872: Maps). This work on the wall suggests a state of some prosperity.

La Maddaremmeng's support for a firmer form of Islam and a quarrel with his mother over this matter are clearly important, but no details are given, though we know these from other sources.[57] This dispute led to an attack on his mother's base at Pattiro, which in turn led to another attack from Gowa under its new ruler, Sultan Malikussaid. The chronicle records succinctly that La Maddaremmeng was defeated, and that he fled to southern Luwu, but was captured, brought to Makassar and exiled to Siang. The Dutch and Makasar sources provide a much fuller picture

56 This attempted marriage is also recorded in the Gowa chronicle (Cummings 2007: 46).

57 Noorduyn (1955: 116) explains that the dispute concerned the question of whether Muslims not born into slavery could be kept in slavery, or whether, following some Islamic opinion, they had to be freed, as La Maddaremmeng believed. Andaya (1981: 40) sees this as an attack on Sufism, but the question deserves further research. There is a Makasar *sinrili'* (or literary work) dealing with this dispute between La Maddaremmeng and his mother in NBG 78, of which we have a transcription in the Cense papers (Leiden University Library, Mss D Or. 545, Item 75, d).

and allow us to date these events.[58] *The Makassar Annals* tell us that Malikussaid returned victorious to Gowa on 19 November 1643 and La Maddaremmeng arrived on 23 July 1644. He was not exiled to Siang until 19 June 1646 (Cummings 2010: 62–6).

The chronicle then moves back in time to deal with the revolt of La Tenriaji To Senrima, the younger brother of La Maddaremmeng, who seems to have fled to southern Luwu with his brother but managed to return to Bone. Again, we know from *The Makassar Annals* that Sultan Malikussaid left Makassar on 18 April 1646 to deal with this rebellion, inflicted a devastating defeat on Bone at Pasémpe' and returned home on 25 May 1646 (Cummings 2010: 62–6).[59] To Senrima and other Bone nobles were taken back to Gowa. It is not clear whether To Senrima was exiled to Siang at the same time as his brother, but the chronicle tells us he died there.

The final section of the chronicle is again not strictly in chronological order. It begins with the appointment of a Bone nobleman, To Bala, to oversee the governance of Bone; this appointment actually took place at the same time as Malikussaid returned to Gowa in 1643. There is some difference in the sources about the nature of To Bala's appointment and his relationship with the senior Gowa noble, Karaeng riSumanna' (Andaya 1981: 41–2; Cummings 2007: 49), but he seems to have weathered the crisis of To Senrima's revolt in 1646 and stayed in place for 17 years, until 1660. On 7 August 1660, he too fled from the indignity inflicted on Bone's labourers, including the nobility, digging defence ditches in Gowa and went into revolt. Three days later, an army from Gowa set out in pursuit; a little over a month later, this army defeated the Bone forces and To Bala was killed (Cummings 2010: 88–9).

It is only at this point that the chronicle introduces Arung Palakka, Matinroé riBontala', as an actor, though his genealogy has been set out in the previous chapter. It is possible he was brought to Gowa from Soppeng as a hostage as early as 1644 (Andaya 1981: 51), but he had joined To Bala and is reputed to have shown bravery and skill in eluding capture. He now appears leading a remnant force of Bone troops off to relative safety on Butung, which can be dated to 25 December 1660 (Cummings 2010: 90).

58 This period of history has received much attention from Speelman's *Notitie* onwards. Useful modern accounts are Noorduyn (1955); Andaya (1981); and, with particular reference to Bone, Abdurrazak et al. (1995) and Palloge (2006).

59 Andaya (1981: 42) wrongly dates this revolt to 1644.

The statement that it was this action that ended Bone's enslavement to Gowa is significant; it is his involvement that marks the beginning of successes to come.

The chronicle has no detail on the next seven years except that Bone was under the control of Arung Amali, an official appointed by Gowa. Late in 1667, he was ordered to take reinforcements for the army of Gowa under the command of Karaeng Bontomarannu, which was besieging Butung. There they met Arung Palakka and large numbers of troops went over to the side of Arung Palakka and the Dutch under Speelman. On 4 January 1667, Karaeng Bontomarannu and the other leaders of Gowa's forces surrendered to the Dutch (Andaya 1981: 76–7).

Even allowing for the need to restrict the focus of the chronicle to 'the land of Bone and the ruling of Bone', this is a very thin coverage of the eventful years between La Maddaremmeng's accession in 1630 and early 1667, to say nothing of the attempt to reinstall La Maddaremmeng as ArumPone recorded in *The Makassar Annals* for 7 February 1667, which is passed over entirely (Cummings 2010: 101). As far as the chronicle is concerned, La Maddaremmeng had ceased being ArumPone at least by the time of his exile to Siang in 1646. As discussed in Section 8, this treatment of La Maddaremmeng's reign is relevant to the date and circumstance of the creation of the chronicle.

Plate 1 The first page of the chronicle text as found in manuscript NBG 101 in the Leiden University Libraries

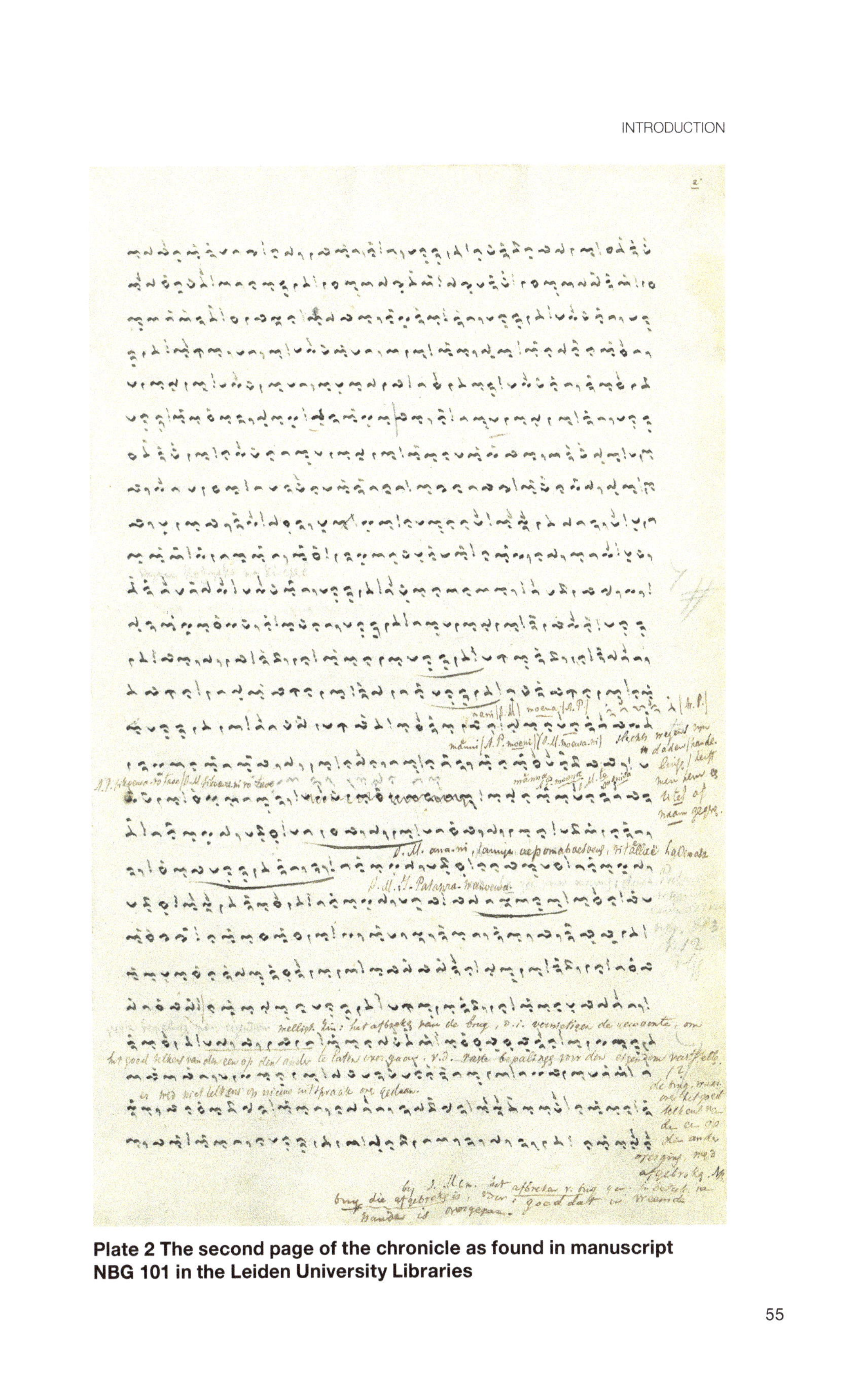

Plate 2 The second page of the chronicle as found in manuscript NBG 101 in the Leiden University Libraries

Appendix 1: Other manuscript versions of the chronicle

In Section 3 of the Introduction, the manuscript from which this diplomatic edition of the chronicle has been derived is described and, in Section 4, the reasons for choosing to present a diplomatic edition and the choice of the version found in NBG 101 are set out. This appendix surveys a selection of other versions of the work.

The most important point to come out of this survey is the confirmation of the status of the chronicle as a *work* in the sense defined in Section 2 of the Introduction. In this appendix, we describe a version as 'complete' if it conforms to the beginning and end of the NBG 101 version and contains most of the same content. Where a version is incomplete or contains additional material, especially at the end, there is usually a reason for this, and the version can be seen as a variant form of the work.

The survey is necessarily selective in several ways. The Bugis manuscript tradition contains a vast miscellany of historical information about Bone, much of it relating to the period covered by the chronicle. There are king lists, treaty texts, episodes, legal material and so on. The total quantity of manuscript material relating in one way or another to the history of Bone is probably at least equivalent to that for the history of Wajo as set out by Noorduyn (1955: 21–31) and even that exhaustive listing is by no means complete. The material described below is limited to that concerned with the chronicle, understood as a work.

The survey is also selective because life is short and the thorough cataloguing of Bugis manuscripts demands much patience and knowledge. We hope, however, that we have handled and consulted most of the older versions of the chronicle. We have had access to microfilm copies of the majority, as noted for particular manuscripts below. A major omission in our search for further versions has been the microfilm material held in the Arsip Nasional Republik Indonesia (National Archives of Indonesia) office in Makassar and listed in Mukhlis et al. (2003). Searching through this list, there are dozens of potentially relevant items, but most probably date from the twentieth century or have been covered in other ways. Undoubtedly, there are also versions in privately owned manuscripts across South Sulawesi that are not yet recorded.

As Macknight and Caldwell (2001) explain, the very nature of Bugis (and Makasar) literacy precludes the possibility of a neat stemma of manuscripts in a demonstrable phylogenetic relationship with each other, other than in exceptional cases. We have tried, in some detail, to compare variant versions of the chronicle, but the critical method, or *recensio*, does not work to produce a more 'reliable' version of the text. Alternatively, Macknight and Caldwell (2001: 151) suggest looking for groups of manuscripts and instance this work as an example of this procedure. Cummings (2007: 15–16) comes to very similar conclusions in respect of the manuscript versions of the Gowa chronicle.

Four other manuscript versions of the Bone chronicle form a group with NBG 101: NBG 100, Bone 5, Bone 20 and Andaya 2. These five manuscripts are distinguished by a combination of features, some of which are shared by other manuscripts, but not in combination. The common features are:

- Words are not divided, although this is common to many manuscripts. At least with NBG 101, NBG 100 and Bone 5, there are similarities in the handwriting.
- The codex does not contain significant other material in the Makasar language or relating directly to Gowa and cannot be shown to have been written in Makassar. The overall focus of the contents of each manuscript is on Bugis states, especially Bone.
- Although there is material missing in some when compared with the text of NBG 101, there is no additional material.
- They agree on one difficult point in the text: the phrase *aja' mumarullé* occurs towards the end of Chapter 1, where the first ruler gathers the people of Bone and tells them: 'Do not wriggle about.' All other versions have variant readings.

A less clear group consists of NBG 208, Berlin 386 and Rylands Makassar 2. They all appear to be miscellanies of items in both Bugis and Makasar put together for non-local readers with various decorative touches. They date to various times during the nineteenth century and were probably copied in Makassar. There are significant textual differences between them, at least in terms of the chronicle, and Rylands Makassar 2, in particular, has some particular readings and content. This shows the range of material available to a scribe in Makassar in the nineteenth century. Further conclusions would require comparisons of all other items in a codex with other versions of each item.

Manuscripts are listed by the location of the original, where this is clear, or by the location of the microfilm or photocopy, if the whereabouts of the original is not known. Each item has been given a tag, such as NBG 99, for easy reference. The tag 'MAK' is used for the collection of the former Matthesstichting (Matthes Foundation) in Makassar, now the Yayasan Kebudayaan Sulawesi Selatan dan Tenggara (South and Southeast Sulawesi Cultural Foundation). The remaining original manuscripts of this collection are held in the office of the National Archives in Makassar. There are also microfilm copies of many items from the collection, including many items otherwise lost. Microfilm copies of manuscripts in the library of The Australian National University are noted; the Macknight reels are a series of microfilms held under the general title of 'South Celebes manuscripts—Naskah-naskah Sulawesi Selatan'.

Leiden

Leiden University Libraries (Universitaire Bibliotheken Leiden) Southeast Asian Special Collections Loan collection of manuscripts from Dutch Bible Society (Nederlands Bijbelgenootschap)

NBG 99

This is the base manuscript Matthes used for his edition of the chronicle—and other works—in the *Boegineesche Chrestomathie* (1864, 1872). It contains numerous linguistic notes, textual annotations and instructions to the printer, including marks for word division in the text, which, as written, does not divide words. The Bugis text is written on every third line, leaving space for interlinear comments, and the whole manuscript seems to have been produced for Matthes to work on. It is a large folio codex; the pages measure 39.5 x 25 cm, with an internal text covering 32 x 18 cm—apparently an account book of some kind. The text covers 290 pages with only 14 lines of text to the page. There are many blank pages after the text. It is on European paper, with no apparent watermark.

The chronicle starts at the top of page 171 and ends on page 217, line 4. The handwriting is clear and a little freer than that in NBG 101. The contents are listed by Matthes (1875: 32–5) and relevant items are included in Noorduyn's (1955: 21–31) list of material relating to Wajo. There is a microfilm copy in the ANU Library.

NBG 100

As Matthes (1875: 38) explains, he obtained this manuscript from Aru Padali, ruler of Tempe, and it is probably the manuscript he received in November 1861 (van den Brink 1943: 214). The text of the chronicle begins at the top of page 1 and ends at page 18, line 25. On page 14, in the middle of line 24, the text jumps about three pages in a clear scribal error; in NBG 101, this is from page 14, line 10, to page 17, line 11, which is from Chapter 8 to Chapter 11.

The text covers 194 folio pages, with 29 lines to the page and no division of words. Pages measure 34 x 21.5 cm and the internal text measures 30 x 17 cm. The watermark is Pro Patria in Dutch garden and L v Gerrevink. There are many blank pages after the text. A few pages from the end, there is further text with a date of AH 1273 (1856–57 CE). Matthes (1875: 38–9) describes the text as 'neatly and clearly written'—the same terms he uses for NBG 101—and the handwriting is indeed very similar and possibly by the same scribe. There are also many similarities in content to NBG 101, as listed by Matthes (1875: 35–8), and these are marked in the margin. Relevant items are included in Noorduyn's (1955: 21–31) list of material relating to Wajo. There is a microfilm copy in the ANU Library.

NBG 101

See Section 3 of the Introduction to this volume.

NBG 131

A complete version of the chronicle text begins on page 35, line 1, and runs with 27 lines to the page to the bottom of page 57. A further sentence, which runs over into the first line of page 58, deals succinctly with Arung Palakka's conquest of Tiworo and his return to Makassar. See Gaynor (2016: 97–106) for a detailed account of these events. There are also some further minor expansions of the text such as the names of all five children of the *tomanurung* on page 37. There is extensive annotation, apparently by Matthes.

There are 115 pages of text, followed by about 20 blank pages. There are 27 lines to the page. Pages measure 33 x 20.5 cm, with an internal text of 26 x 16.5 cm, and watermark Pro Patria in Dutch garden over JH&Z, and J. Honig & Zoon. There is no word division. Contents are listed by Matthes (1875: 53). It contains other historical material about Bone, some items in Makasar and a copy of a Wajo chronicle listed as C2 by Noorduyn (1955: 23). There is a microfilm copy in the ANU Library.

NBG 208

A large folio codex containing a miscellany of historical items in both Makasar and Bugis. Matthes (1881: 6–16) distinguishes 183 items in its 254 pages. Pages measure 43.5 x 21.5 cm, with an internal text of 27 x 15 cm, and 31 lines to the page. There is no watermark. A final colophon records that Tajuddin completed the manuscript on 18 February 1877. Taken as a whole, the codex has the appearance of a compilation of historical material made in Makassar for a scholar interested in local history. It may even have been intended for Matthes, who completed his duties as director of the training school in Makassar in October 1879, about three weeks after Tajuddin died (Matthes 1881: 23; van den Brink 1943: 162).

The material relating to the Bone chronicle begins on page 95 and runs to page 132. This includes material on the rulers of Palakka and lists of ArumPone up to 1860. The text is neatly laid out in paragraphs, with the first word of a new page quoted at the bottom of the preceding page. There is no division of words.

There is a microfilm copy in the ANU Library.

F.Or.A9

A negative microfilm. A positive microfilm copy is also held in the ANU Library. A note in the first frame reads: 'Ex bibliotheca Regis Goa in insula Celebes.' The present whereabouts of the original is not known. A complete version of the chronicle is found at page 140, line 1, to page 173, line 15. In his unpublished notes held with the microfilm, Cense describes this section as

> a piece of the history of Bone more or less agreeing with the text in the Boeginesche Chrestomathie, only here and there somewhat fuller, e.g. in this manuscript the children of the Manurung are names where they are lacking in the Chrestomathie.

The manuscript is written in several hands with a traditional palm-leaf quill in heavy black ink. The section starting from page 140 and ending at page 256, which deals first with this chronicle and then with some more detailed episodes in the history of Bone from the earliest times until the eighteenth century, and finally with a chronicle of Wajo, seems all to be by the same hand. For this section, there are 17 lines to the page. There is no word division. An earlier item claims to have been written in 1793 CE (page 89), which provides a *terminus post quem* for the later sections.

Noorduyn (1955: 22–3) makes important use of this manuscript as his C1.

F.Or.A42a [MAK 8]

The chronicle begins on page 1, line 14, directly after a colophon with the date of 1830 CE. It is not clear how this date relates to the actual manuscript, which appears to be a standard Matthes Foundation copy made in the 1930s with 38 lines per page. The enclosed contents list says it has been copied from a manuscript belonging to 'A. Pan[?] in Tanete'. The chronicle text, which concludes on page 16, line 24, is a poor text, with some significant omissions as well as much minor variation. Words are divided, but with many errors.

A microfilm in Leiden appears to be the only record of Item 8 from the Matthes Foundation collection. There is also a microfilm copy in the ANU Library.

Berlin

Berlin State Library (Staatsbibliothek Preussischer Kulturbesitz) Ms. orient. fol. 386

Berlin 386

A fine volume with a book plate containing the arms and name of A.W. Schlegel von Gottleben, whose death in 1845 presumably provides a latest date for the item. A date of 1729 appears on page 3 with a comment that this is 226 years after the disappearance of Makkalempié.

It has 162 pages, measuring 29.8 x 19.4 cm, with 21 lines of text written within c. 25 x 15.5 cm. The watermark is IWB and VI, with Dutch garden and Pro Patria.

The chronicle text begins on page 6, line 1, and runs to page 47, line 15, with nothing further on the page. There is no word division. Some sections are introduced by several lines in red and with expanded spacing, and some names are also in red. The contents are listed by Matthes (1875: 99–101). The codex contains a miscellany of Bugis and Makasar historical and religious works in both Lontara' and Arabic scripts. The Bone chronicle is the longest item. There is a clear interest in Bone and Matthes argues that the copyist was Bugis. The Bone chronicle text is generally close to NBG 101. Cummings (2007: 14) describes the material relating to Gowa in this codex.

There is a microfilm copy in the ANU Library.

Manchester

John Rylands University Library

Makassar 2

The Bone chronicle begins at the top of page 37, with the heading 'attoriolongngé riBoné'. The usual text runs to the To Bala defeat at page 85, line 16, and then continues to page 89, line 6, with an account of Arung Palakka's escape from demeaning service in Gowa and eventual flight from Pallетté in Bone to Butung and eventually to 'Jakettara'. This alternative ending throws more light on the early career of Arung Palakka, but also has the effect of omitting any mention of the seven years of Arung Amali's role in Bone and of the events in and around Butung in 1666–67 involving not just Arung Palakka, but also the Dutch East India Company.

The codex of 110 pages, measuring 20.3 x 15.8 cm on blue European paper, also contains a version of the Gowa chronicle and four Malay *hikayat*. The Bugis script is very clear with no word division, but much underlining marks many words. A series of large Roman numerals heads the sections of successive rulers; the series begins in the preceding version of the Gowa chronicle and continues from IX to XXIII for the Bone chronicle. On page 89, there is then a colophon saying that the copying of this item concluded in Kampong Melayu, Makassar, on Wednesday, 7 September 1859. A similar colophon on page 35 dates the completion of copying of the Gowa chronicle to 31 August 1859.

The mixed contents and clear script suggest the codex was prepared for a European collector in the nineteenth century. It was in Britain by 1901. It is described and the contents are listed in Ricklefs and Voorhoeve (1977: 100).

Jakarta

National Library of the Republic of Indonesia (Perpustakaan Nasional Republik Indonesia) VT Collection [Verschillende talen or Miscellaneous languages]

VT 84

A fairly complete version of the chronicle text begins in the middle of page 281 (bottom nine lines) and runs with 25 lines to the page, to page 308 (19 lines). The writing is clear and confident, with a tendency to add fancy swirls. Words are defined by spaces. *Pallawa* are indicated by both three dots and a stroke. At the bottom of right-hand pages, a tag of several *aksara* is given for the top of the succeeding page. Many personal names are underlined, and most reigns are marked with Arabic and Roman numerals in the margin.

In addition to the usual minor variations from NBG 101, there are more significant differences. On page 298, after the account of the treaty at Timurung, there is a diagram of three sets of four concentric circles named as the three states. Soppeng has a strange hernia-like protrusion. The names and an explanatory caption are additions to the NBG 101 text. There is also a significant omission. At page 302, line 9, the text jumps from NBG 101, page 15, line 22, to page 16, line 20. This gap of about a page probably represents the copyist jumping from one page to another in his model.

The manuscript is noted in Behrend (1998: 316) and a detailed contents list is given by Cense (n.d.: 3–4). Cense gives the dimensions as 33 x 21 cm. This is a substantial codex of 394 pages containing the usual miscellany of historical, legal and religious materials, including other historical information on Bone and much on Soppeng. The name 'Perné Pinrang' inside the cover suggests a European owner at some point. There is a microfilm copy in the ANU Library and a digital version on the Perpustakaan Nasional website.

VT 124

A complete version of the chronicle text begins on page 8, line 1, and runs with 25 lines to the page, to page 32, line 17. There is no word division.

The manuscript is noted in Behrend (1998: 318) and a detailed contents list is given by Cense (n.d.: 5–6). Cense gives the dimensions as 31.5 x 20 cm. This is a codex of 96 pages containing mainly historical material. From page 47, it is in Makasar. There is a microfilm copy in the ANU Library (Macknight, Reel 21, Item 5) and a digital version on the Perpustakaan Nasional website. See also Cummings (2007: 14) on this manuscript.

Watampone, South Sulawesi

Various locations

Bone 1

A complete chronicle text starts at the top of page 19A, with a preliminary title in a circle, and runs, with 36 lines to the page, to page 27A, line 23. It is clearly written with some names picked out in larger script and many emendations. Words are consistently divided.

The manuscript consists of folders loosely bound between red cardboard covers. Pages are numbered by double-page spread and the same number is found in the left and right upper corners of each spread. There are 135 spreads—that is, 270 pages, measuring 32.5 x 21 cm. There is a contents list for the usual variety of items, many of historical interest.

On the initial flyleaf, the manuscript is described as 'Lontara Keradjaan Bone'. It is said to belong to A. Muh. Ali, and to have been copied in 1947 from a manuscript owned by Andi Paworeki Petta Renring. This statement is signed by A. Muh. Ali. There is also a stamp of the Bone Kantor Kebudayaan (Cultural Office). In 1972, when the manuscript was filmed, A. Muh. Ali was the head of that office. Many items are headed in modern Indonesian and there are various inserted notes and guides, such as a typed list of Dutch officials in Bone from 1905 to 1948. This manuscript is the product of a person with modern Indonesian literacy and a strong interest in local history, very probably A. Muh. Ali himself. The ANU Library holds the microfilm as Macknight (Reel 8, Item 1).

Bone 5

The chronicle text starts at the top of page 2, though a substantial portion of the top of the page has been torn away, affecting the first five lines. It then continues, with 31 lines to the page, to the bottom of page 15, where it ends with a statement in Bugis that this is the end of the work and an elaborate *tammat* and Arabic phrase. The handwriting is mostly small and clear, with some sections—apparently random—in a larger hand. This variation is seen in other items in the codex. There is no word division in the text.

The codex, in a fine embossed brown leather cover, runs to 162 pages, measuring 33 x 20.5 cm. The front flyleaves claim it is owned by Andi Pabbara and by Petta Lolo Mappaseling/Andi Mappaseling. In 1972, it was manuscript Number 5 in the Cultural Office in Watampone when it was filmed and the microfilm is now to be found in the ANU Library (Macknight, Reel 8, Item 2). In May 1982, photocopies of the codex were made by Muh. Salim, one of which, entitled 'Lontarak attoriolong riBone', is also held in the ANU Library. A card captured in the photocopy of what seems to be a cover notes that the manuscript was registered on 15 IV 1974, but the significance of this is unknown.

A contents list, in both typescript and handwriting, contains 146 items, mainly of historical interest, but with much else besides.

Bone 20

This is a good example of a fragment of the chronicle text. This begins on page 91, line 1, and runs to page 99, line 15, with nothing further on the page. This covers from the beginning of the chronicle to near the end of Chapter 3, where it ends abruptly at the equivalent in NBG 101 of page 6, line 4 up.

The manuscript contains 105 pages of clear text, as well as various notes. Pages 14 and 15 are missing. There is a table of contents in the front showing most items are concerned with Bone. Pages measure 27 x 18.5 cm, with 19 lines to the page. There is no word division. The paper appears to date from the nineteenth century, although no watermark is apparent. The front cover, the flyleaf and the torn original cover all contain the name Andi Rajeng Petta Lebbi', presumably as the owner. The name of A. Muh. Ali also appears on the front cover.

The manuscript was filmed in 1978 at the house of Muh. Rafi in Watampone and the microfilm is held by the ANU Library as Macknight (Reel 24, Item 1).

Canberra

ANU Library

Andaya 2

An almost complete chronicle text starts on page 31, line 14, and runs to page 48, line 31, where the text ends with the death of Matinroé riTallo'. Another item begins immediately, and it is not clear why the text ends at this point. The handwriting is slightly clumsy, but usually clear. Words are divided, if not always accurately. Occasional deletions and corrections suggest the scribe was following a model, though not necessarily precisely. There are many minor differences from the NBG 101 text.

This codex is the second of a series of six photocopied volumes obtained by Dr Leonard Andaya in 1976 and lodged in the ANU Library. Pages are numbered in heavy figures at the top of the page. The numbering begins at page 27 and runs to page 140; it seems these 113 pages reflect a fragment of an original codex.

Appendix 2: Absolute reign dates

The chronicle contains no absolute dates and we may assume that chronological comparisons with other places did not interest its author. Given the availability of some absolute dates in Makasar sources, at least for the seventeenth century, this avoidance of absolute dating in the chronicle may even be, as Noorduyn (1965: 141–2) suggests, a deliberate stylistic choice. In any event, the interests of modern historians require that some attempt be made to estimate dates, if only for successive reigns.

Noorduyn (1965: 148–52) has made a helpful start on the matter. He discusses whether the chronicle uses solar or lunar years and concludes that, in the seventeenth century, it is more likely lunar years were intended. This does not necessarily apply, however, for the period before Muslim influence, and, for Bone, that may be somewhat later than on the west coast. Another issue is whether the number of years for a reign as given in the chronicle refers to completed years or years begun—that is, does a reign of '10 years' mean somewhere between 120 and 131 months or between 108 and 119 months? Another possibility, although unlikely, is that it means a reign has lasted 10 times past some particular season or point on the calendar.

These factors prevent any precise conclusions, especially for the earlier reigns, but the range of possibilities is not great. It is also easiest to use solar years and the common era in the following discussion.

The chronicle provides the length of most reigns and, if we accept these as accurate, this allows counting back from a known point. A firm base is found in the short reign of the eleventh ArumPone, La Tenrirua, in 1611.

(Dates for later rulers are given in the commentary in the Introduction to this volume.) The following discussion works backwards from 1611, using the conventional ordinal numbers for each ArumPone.

10. Wé Tenritappu 9 years 1602 to 1611

This fits with the various events of her reign.

9. La Pattawé 7 years 1595 to 1602

8. La Icca' 11 years 1584 to 1595

The first difficulty arises with the reign of Bongkangngé, for which no figure is given in the chronicle. A likely solution is given in a king list in the manuscript known as Berlin 386 (page 2), which gives reign lengths, beginning with the fifth ArumPone, Mappajungngé, and running to the fifteenth ArumPone in the eighteenth century. The fact that all other reign lengths agree with what is otherwise known gives some support for the figure of 30 years for Bongkangngé.

7. Bongkangngé 30 years 1554 to 1584

This also serves to date the Tellumpoccoé treaty to 1582 and a long reign allows for the many events recorded.

6. Boté'é 25 years before abdicating 1529 to 1554

This span comfortably covers the accession of Tunipalangga as ruler of Gowa, which Cummings (2007: 109) dates to 1546 and which occurs during this reign.

5. Mappajungngé 27 years 1502 to 1529

The chronicle does not provide a reign length for Mappajungngé's mother, Makkalempié. She was presumably adult when her elderly father died and, given she bore nine children, she probably lived into her 30s, at least. There is no way to discover, however, whether she was married and had children before or after her accession as ArumPone. Her eldest child was aged either 11 or 19 at the time of her abdication, and she then lived for a further four years. A reasonable estimate for her reign is 20 years.

In Berlin 386 (page 3), there is a note under the date 1729 that this is 226 years since the disappearance of Makkalempié—that is, she disappeared in 1503. This, in turn, dates her abdication to 1499.

4.	**Makkalempié**	[20 years]	1482 to 1502
3.	**Kerrampélua'**	72 years	1410 to 1482

The chronicle does not provide a reign length for La Ummasa', the uncle of Kerrampélua'. He had adult sons when Kerrampélua' was born, but they may have been born before his accession, and he lived a further 17 years after abdicating. A shorter estimate of 10 years for his actual reign seems appropriate.

2.	**La Ummasa'**	[10 years]	1400 to 1410
1.	**Matasilompo'é**	32 years	1368 to 1400

These dates, especially those in the fourteenth and fifteenth centuries, should not be taken as precisely accurate, for the reasons explained above. This uncertainty is compounded by comparison with three other attempts to provide absolute dates. While the chronicle is the best-known work dealing with the history of early Bone, it is not the only tradition found in the manuscripts, though the sources on which the two following chronologies are based are not known.

The first set of absolute dates is provided on a large hanging chart, setting out the genealogy of successive ArumPone from the first to the 33rd, who reigned from 1946 to 1951, and then various *bupati* up to A. Muh. Idris Galigo S.H., who was in office until 2013. This chart is currently in the museum in Watampone. The dates on this chart agree with those on an earlier version drawn up in 1968 by A. Pabbara. It was filmed by Macknight in 1972 and is to be found in Macknight (Reel 9, Item 6).

The second set of absolute dates is found in Palloge (2006). Endnotes indicate a range of sources, including local manuscripts, but no direct references are given for the absolute dates provided at the conclusion of the account of each reign.

There is no problem in either source with later dates, and only reigns before 1611 are listed here, in reverse order, as above.

	ArumPone	Museum genealogy	Palloge (2006)	
10.	Wé Tenritappu	1602 to 1611	1603 to 1611	p. 101
9.	La Pattawé	1595 to 1602	1596 to 1603	p. 98
8.	La Icca'	1584 to 1595	1585 to 1596	p. 97
7.	Bongkangngé	1568 to 1584	1560 to 1585	p. 93
6.	Boté'é	1543 to 1568	1535 to 1560	p. 79
5.	Mappajungngé	1516 to 1543	1509 to 1535	p. 72
4.	Makkalempié	1496 to 1516	1470 to 1509	p. 70
3.	Kerrampélua'	1424 to 1496	1398 to 1470	p. 67
2.	La Ummasa'	1358 to 1424	1370 to 1398	p. 61
1.	Matasilompo'é	1326 to 1358	c. 1330 to 1370	p. 56

The third attempt to provide absolute dates is that by Crawfurd (1820), mentioned in Section 9 of the Introduction.

No way of resolving the many inconsistencies in these lists currently presents itself, though some further confirmations may be found by analysing the historical traditions of other kingdoms.

Appendix 3: Placenames in the chronicle

The names of locations in South Sulawesi have been reasonably stable from the period dealt with in the chronicle until the present. That means most placenames in the chronicle can be reliably located in the modern landscape. The chief difficulty arises from the frequent use of some common descriptive names, such as Tanété, meaning a ridge or higher ground. Names are also rendered on maps with many minor variations.

Most of the peninsula is covered by two series of 1:50,000 maps. The first was produced by the Dutch topographical services between 1922 and 1934 (these maps were republished in 1943, mainly by the US Army). The second series was produced by Badan Koordinasi Survei dan Pemetaan Nasional (Bakosurtanal) Geospatial Information Agency/National Mapping Agency of Indonesia in the early 1990s. The placenames of minor villages on Map 2 have been located by reference to these two series of maps, supported by some local knowledge.

The rendition of placenames on the maps in the text follows the principle used in the translation, even when that involves some inconsistencies. Well-known names, usually of larger localities, are given in their Indonesian form; other names, usually of minor settlements, are given in their Bugis form.

The account of the reign of the third ArumPone in Chapter 3 contains groups of placenames that deserve special attention. In the following lists, those names marked with an asterisk [*] cannot be reliably identified, although often their general location is clear from the context. The remainder are shown on Map 2.

Placenames in Chapter 3

Names associated with Kerrampélua' himself

Bone
Palakka
Paccing
Majang
Bukaka
Panyula'
Lipenno

Names of the three standards

1. Woromponong

Majang
*Mata-Anging (this might be the common name Matoanging)
Bukaka-Tengnga
Kawerrang
Palléngoreng
*Mallari
Matajang

2. Right standard

Paccing
*Tanété (a very common name)
*Lémo-Lémo
Masallé
Macégé
Bélawa
*Ciung

3. Left standard

*Araseng
Ujung
Poncéng
Ta'
*Katumpi' (the events described in the following reign suggest this is near Cina and Laliddong)

*Padaccengnga
*Madello'

Conquests of Kerrampélua'

Palléngoreng
*Sinri
Anrobiring
Lémpang
Mellé
*Sancénreng
Cirowali
Apala
Bakke'
*Tanété
*Attassalo (this means 'south of river', but it is not clear which river is meant)
Soga
Lampoko
Lémoape'
Bulu'-Riattassalo
Parippung
*Lompu

Places adopted or merged with Bone under Kerrampélua'

Palakka
*Five territories east of the forest (the word *ale'*, translated here as 'forest', may refer to the hilly region inland of the 100 m contour)
*Babauaé
Barebbo
Pattiro
Cinennung
Ureng
Pasémpe'
Kaju
Ponré
*Nine standards south of the forest
*Nine standards north of the forest

Macknight (1983) argues the 'conquests' reflect an expansion of wet rice agriculture, while those places 'adopted' or 'merged' indicate a more general widening of power. The former lie on the plain between the Gulf of Bone and the edge of the hills, marked on Map 2 by the 100 m contour. The latter are either further from Bone or within the hills.

The Bugis Chronicle of Bone: English text

1

This work tells of the land of Bone and the ruling of Bone. All that there is now for hearing is what the old men tell.

May my belly not swell,[1] may I not weaken, I will not part (from life), telling the names of the monarchs. A sun-shield extends a shadow over children of the splendid ones.[2] Thus I seek approval before going on to set out in order the lineage of the ruling sovereigns.

There were kings, so the story goes, back in (the age of I La) Galigo,[3] but then no longer was there anyone called king. For the people did not know how to discuss things with each other. The people just ate each other like fish do. They were selling each other all the time (as slaves). There was no longer customary order, let alone what might be called law. It is said that for the space of seven generations there was no king.[4] For this same time also the people did not know how to discuss things with each other, nowhere was there customary order, nowhere law.

---

1 This is a standard formula that occurs repeatedly to excuse the author for using the personal name of high-status individuals. Here it heads a list of similar phrases in a general deflection of ill consequence.

2 The protection of a sun-shield or umbrella is a mark of nobility or high status. All those of appropriate descent share in this benefit according to their level of status. The exculpatory phrases can be taken to apply at all levels of status.

3 Refer to the commentary in the Introduction for discussion of La Galigo and other themes in this paragraph.

4 The figure of seven generations is probably conventional, for whatever reason, rather than literal.

This, then, is how there began to be kings. It happened one day that the lightning and thunder raged together,[5] the land also shook, it is said to have continued like this for one week.[6] When the lightning, thunder and the earthquake had ceased, suddenly there was a man to be seen in the middle of the field. He was all in white. So it came about that the people gathered together, each according to his area. Then it was agreed by all the people to call him *tomanurung*.[7] So it came about that all the people were of one view. Then they agreed to go together to attach themselves to this man whom they called *tomanurung*. They went there. The common people said, 'Here we have come to you, blessed one.[8] Have mercy on us children. Do not disappear. You have settled in your land. You have us as slaves. Your wish is what we wish. Whatever the orders, we will execute them. Even our children and our wives, (if) you reject them, we also reject them in turn. If you stay here, then we will make you lord.'

After that, this man who was called *tomanurung* said, 'That is good, friends. I just say this to you. I am not able to be king, since I am but a slave. But if you wish to have a lord, there is my lord. You make him lord if you want to.'

All the people said, 'How do we know how we make lord someone we do not see?'

He who was called *tomanurung* said, 'If you really want it, I will show him to you.'

All the people said, 'That is indeed our wish. Be faithful in your mercy and in showing us the way.'

Following that, all the people were shown the way to what is called Matajang. Again thunder and lightning raged together when they reached Matajang. They came and saw the *tomanurung* sitting on the flat stone. He was all in yellow. Sitting together with the person of the king, there was one holding his umbrella, a yellow umbrella,[9] one fanned him, one carried his *sirih* box.

---

5 Literally, they ate each other.

6 That is, for seven days. The figure of seven is again probably significant.

7 *Tomanurung* means, literally, 'descended one'—that is, a person who has come down from the upper world. See Section 7 of the Introduction for further discussion.

8 This phrase is in the form of a masculine personal name with the preceding *La*.

9 The yellow umbrella is a sign of royalty.

When they came there to the *tomanurung*, the *tomanurung* said, 'There you are, old man.'[10]

The old man said, 'Yes, lord.'

After that, all the people knew that the man who had been called king was nothing more than an old man. He who had been called *tomanurung* said, 'Again, I acknowledge my lord.'

Following that, all the people went to the *tomanurung* all in yellow. All the people said, 'Here we come to you, lord.[11] We want you to have mercy (on us), and to establish yourself here in your land. Do not disappear. You we will make lord. Your wish is what we wish, just as commands are. Even our children and wives, (if) you reject them, we also reject them in turn. If only you will stay here, then you will have us as slaves. You will protect us against lack of food.'[12]

The *tomanurung* said, 'Your thoughts are not double. You do not lie.'

Following that, all the people approved the words of the *tomanurung*. The (*to*)*manurung* was led back to Bone. Then that (*to*)*manurung* ruled in Bone, and a royal hall was set up. The royal hall was completed and the (*to*)*manurung* was taken up to sit in the royal hall. For that (*to*)*manurung* no report is heard about his personal name. Only for his deeds is he given a title. If he saw the plain full of people, he looked down on them and he just knew immediately how many people there were. Thus he was just given the title, may my belly not swell, Matasilompo'é <the Eye of the whole plain>.[13]

Matasilompo'é married in Toro' with the (*to*)*manurung* of Toro', may my belly not swell. Their children were La Ummasa', may my belly not swell, and someone called, may I not be parted (from life), La Pattanrawanua[14]

10 'Old man' is a literal translation. The word also has connotations of political and social rank.

11 In this speech, which closely follows that addressed to the earlier figure, the honorific second person is used (except where it might cause confusion with the exclusive first-person plural). The contrast between the ordinary second-person forms in the previous speech and the honorific here is undoubtedly intentional.

12 The full sense is: 'You will be our protection against the small birds [*dongi'*] that infest rice fields, so that we are not left with empty ears of paddy.'

13 The sense of this name may be that he was able to see the whole of the area under his control. This implies that Bone was still very limited in extent.

14 Despite the masculine *La*, this is certainly a daughter, as shown by her later marriage. This use of *La* is not as anomalous in a title—as this name seems to be—as it would be in a personal name.

<Marker out of territory>, by name. There were five in their family. As for the other names, they remain in records which are rolled up.[15] This work only tells of the succession of events in Bone in their proper order.

As for the works of the *(to)manurung* who ruled in Bone, he first set up what is called bridge breaking. He regularised the exchange of goods for both parties. The person who has possession of goods, they all definitely belong together to the person. It is in good faith that they are held and there is no consequent litigation. He also set up precedents, laws and customary order. They were then followed. This *(to)manurung* also owned the Woromporong banner.[16]

When he had completed four eight-year cycles[17] of ruling Bone he gathered together the people of Bone and took leave of them, saying, 'Sit down, friends. Do not wriggle about. This is my child called La Ummasa'. He succeeds me. By him also, I uphold our agreement.'

Following that, there was lightning and there was thunder. Suddenly, the *(to)manurung*, both husband and wife, were no more to be seen in their places. Furthermore it was seen that both the yellow umbrella was no longer to be seen in its keeping place, and the betel box was no more. Only then too was our lord,[18] La Ummasa', by name, may my belly not swell, immediately set up to rule. Also there was no longer an umbrella in Bone.

2

The *(to)manurung* of Matajang begat La Ummasa', also called To Mulaiépanreng <He who first had a grave>. After the disappearance of our lords, both husband and wife, La Ummasa', may my belly not swell, ruled in Bone. Only when he passed on was he called To Mulaiépanreng. When he ruled, only his shield shaded him. If he went forth, he just had

15 This is an important reference to the thin palm-leaf strips coiled up on a device somewhat like a modern cassette recorder tape, which were used for writing before the introduction of paper. See Macknight (2016).

16 This name refers to a cluster, understood as a cluster of stars—that is, the Pleiades.

17 A *pariama* cycle may also run for 12 or 100 years.

18 The first-person possessive, though in singular form in the Bugis, is clearly meant in the plural, as elsewhere in the text.

to go in the sun, for there was no longer an umbrella in Bone. Also he was called Panrébessié <the Ironsmith>. He was also praised for his memory. He was also said to be vigilant. He was also said to be well-balanced.

The sister of ArumPone called <La> Pattanrawanua married the man who was king of Palakka, called La Pattikeng.

Also when (La Ummasa') ruled in Bone, he conquered Biru, he conquered Cellu, he conquered Malloi', he conquered Anrobiring, he conquered Majang. He also quarrelled with his brother-in-law, who was king of Palakka, called La Pattikeng. From both sides there arose a war between the brothers-in-law. After three months of war, neither had been beaten, and they were reconciled with each other. (La Ummasa') too was said to be without match in Bone in his authority, his eminence and his power.[19]

He had no child as heir, although he did, in fact, father To Suallé and To Salawaka, but their mother was only a commoner. When he knew his sister who had married in Palakka to be pregnant, he went to sleep on the problem and it is said he was shown what to do. After that he was relaxed at heart for he knew his sister, who was married in Palakka, was in labour. He called To Suallé and To Salawaka and said, 'Go now quickly westwards to Palakka for my young sister is said to be in labour. If my young sister is delivered, just take the baby in a rough sling,[20] you hold it close, you bring it quickly eastwards to here. Thus its umbilical cord will be cut here, and thus too it will be washed here.'

To Suallé and To Salawaka did indeed hasten and went quickly. They came to Palakka, they went straight on up to the palace. To Suallé and To Salawaka did not even sit down. The wife of the king of Palakka was delivered and her child was a boy. His hair all stood up on end. To Suallé went straight up and took the baby in a rough sling, he held it close in a gathered-up sarong, then he went off eastwards to Bone. But the king of Palakka was absent when his child was taken.

19 These three attributes could also be taken in a purely physical sense to refer to his size, his height and his strength, but the context favours the political connotations.

20 The specific term, *apopang*, refers to a device formed from a folded areca palm leaf. For an illustration, see Matthes (1874b: Plate 15, Item 40).

When they came to Bone, they went straight on up to the royal hall. After that (the baby's) umbilical cord was cut, and after that also, he was washed. ArumPone's sister, called I Samateppa,[21] was ordered to take care of him. I Samateppa looked after her nephew. That very night a general summons was given to the people of Bone, namely, 'Gather yourselves together tomorrow, bringing arms.'

Early the next morning, there were the people of Bone complete with arms. The Woromporong was unfurled. ArumPone went down to the meeting house. ArumPone said, 'For this, have I gathered together all you people of Bone. Here is my child called La Saliwu and entitled Kerrampélua'. To him I hand over the kingship of Bone. By this child of mine also, I uphold the treaty which our lord, before disappearing, entrusted to my hands.'

The people of Bone all gave their assent and after that they rendered fealty and the command was also given to send for the shamans.[22] Immediately, on that very day, the ceremony was set in train. Our lord Kerrampélua' was enthroned by his uncle over seven days and seven nights. Indeed, the person who was holding the baby, so the story goes, was kept awake for seven days and seven nights. When the rites were completed, after that his umbilical cord was carried around the house. When his afterbirth had been carried around the house, our lord, the old one, moved down from the palace.[23]

Our lord Kerrampélua' was called ArumPone. He then lived in the royal hall. His aunt, called I Samateppa, acted as parent to him. Then our lord, the old one, if it happened he wanted to travel, he sent up to his child, saying, 'Go up to your lord. Say it happens that the lord of you (messengers)[24] wants to travel. Give orders to take him.'

21 I Samateppa is not listed among the siblings of La Ummasa' in the other sources referred to in the previous chapter. It is easy to imagine the task of wet nurse being given to a woman of lower status.

22 The shamans or *bissu* are associated with all major traditional ceremonies in Bugis society.

23 Compare the modern Toraja birth ritual as described by Volkman (1985: 50) and Nooy-Palm (1986: 111).

24 That is, La Ummasa'. The use of the possessive covering the first-person plural inclusive and the second-person polite distinguishes this from the normal second-person possessive of the previous sentence.

Then also the holder of the baby, so the story goes, would say, 'Go friends, you call people to go and carry your lord.' This was, so the story goes, how our lord organised it if it happened that he travelled, everything in fact was organised by our lord, the old one.

Seventeen years after he handed over kingship to his nephew, a serious illness struck our lord, the old one, and that carried him off. Then indeed he was called Puatta Mulaiépanreng <Our lord who first had a grave>.

3

Puatta' Mulaiépanreng had as nephew our lord Kerrampélua'. Then our lord Kerrampélua' ruled in Bone. He was already king in the lifetime of his uncle, since on the night of his birth kingship in Bone was handed over to him. At his birth he was enthroned and To Suallé supported him and To Salawaka acted as chancellor. But if there was a legal judgement that was difficult for the judge to decide, it was sent up to the royal hall, and the discussion proceeded in this way. To Suallé held the baby and the people on both sides put their case. To Salawaka sorted out the arguments on both sides. Then the person who was holding the baby, he determined the penalty for the person, that is the person at fault. Yet this decision too was called the judgement of the baby.

When Kerrampélua' had grown up and come of age with women, then he went to Palakka to meet his real parents. As soon as they met when he came to Palakka, he was received by his real parents and was made their heir, and moreover he inherited the market of Palakka. The market of Palakka was brought to Bone and so the people of Bone had a market.

When he went to Palakka to meet his real parents, his marriage was arranged with his first cousin, called Wé Tenriroppo, the daughter and heir of the king of Paccing. They begat, may my belly not swell, (a child) called Wé Benrigau' and entitled Daéng Maroa. As well, she was called Makkalempié. She was also called Bissu riLalempili' <Shaman at court>.[25] She was made queen of Majang. A part of the people of Bukaka were set apart and they were taken to live at Majang and they too were made to be

25 This name may only mean something like 'the Beauty in the royal household', rather than its literal sense.

the people of Makkalempié. A long mansion was erected in Bone and it was called Lawélareng and Makkalempié was also given the name Puatta' riLawélareng <Our lady in La Wélareng>.

Our lord Kerrampélua' was praised as skilful, he was also praised as vigilant, he was also praised as diligent in agriculture, he was also praised as liberal-minded, yet he was not said to be especially clever, none could surpass his bravery for, as the story goes, from his birth fear never affected him and in his age, it is said, he never knew the sensation called fear. Hence he had the name Passoddo' Wakkaé <the Prod of enemies>.

Also he was the first king to give orders to pronounce curses to drive back the enemy if he wanted to raise the war against the enemy, for they are what are called Tuppu-batu <Standing on rock>,[26] but the earlier kings who went back to (La) Galigo had already organised (the conduct of) negotiations as well as of giving orders.

When Kerrampélua' was king, he created two red standards.[27] That is there were the red (standards), two (of them) and the Woromporong, one on its left, one on its right. The people of Bone then divided themselves into three sections. The red (standards) shaded one section (each), the Woromporong shaded one section. It was the Woromporong that shaded the people of Majang and the people of Mata-Anging and the people of Bukaka-Tengnga and the people of Kawerrang and the people of Palléngoreng and the people of Mallari, and the headman of Matajang carried (the standard). It was the red (standard) on the right of the Woromporong that shaded the people of Paccing and the people of Tanété and the people of Lémo-Lémo and the people of Masallé and the people of Macégé' and the people of Bélawa, and Kajao[28] Ciung carried (the standard). It was the red (standard) on the left of the Woromporong that shaded the people of Araseng and the people of Ujung and the people of Poncéng and the people of Ta' and the people of Katumpi' and the people of Padaccengnga and the people of Madello', and Kajao Araseng carried (the standard). ArumPone in person was everywhere at all times, ArumPone gave instructions.

---

26 That is, the curses are made with the full confidence of someone who is, as it were, standing on rock—that is, a noble.

27 Le Roux (1930: 45, and Plate 2) describes and illustrates these.

28 *Kajao* means, literally, old man or, in modern Bugis, old woman.

Our lord Kerrampélua' conquered Palléngoreng, Sinri, Anrobiring. He also conquered Lémpang, Mellé. He also conquered Sancénreng, Cirowali, Apala, Bakke', Tanété, Attassalo, Soga, Lampoko, Lémoape', Bulu'-Riattassalo, Parippung, Lompu.

When he was ruling too, he made one people of the people of Bone and the people of Palakka. The land of Palakka was adopted[29] by Bone. Then it happened that the Limampanua-Rilauale' <Five territories east of the forest> came to merge their land with Bone. Then it also happened that the king of Babauaé, called La Tenriwasu, met his grandson-in-law and made his land merge <with Bone>. ArumPone made one people of the people of Bone and the people of Babauaé. The land of Babauaé was adopted by Bone. Furthermore, it happened that the king of Barebbo came to make his land merge with Bone. The land of Barebbo was adopted by Bone. Then it also happened that the king of Pattiro, called La Paworong, came to meet ArumPone, for they were brothers-in-law, and made his land merge <with Bone>. Then the land of Pattiro was established as a vassal of Bone. Then it also happened that Cinennung, Ureng, Pasémpe' came to merge their lands <with Bone> and the three areas were established <as dependencies>.

Also it happened that the king of Kaju, called La Tenribali, made his land merge with Bone and Kaju was established as a vassal. The king of Kaju too sent an envoy to ask in marriage the child of ArumPone, entitled Makkalempié, may my belly not swell, Wé Benrigau' was her personal name. The king of Kaju was accepted by ArumPone, and after that <the envoy> returned to the territory of the king of Kaju, and so when he had come to his <king's> territory, afterwards the groom proceeded to Bone. Arung Kaju, who was called La Tenribali, wed the child of ArumPone, who was entitled Makkalempié.

Then it also happened that Arung Ponré merged his land with Bone. Then also it happened that all the nine standards[30] south of the forest and all the nine standards north of the forest came to merge their land with Bone. The nine standards south of the forest and the nine standards north of the forest were adopted by Bone. When Kerrampélua' ruled in Bone he conquered the area surrounding Bone.

29 Literally, 'was child to'.

30 'Standard' is used here to mean a village or territory. The usage draws attention to the importance for the ruler of military forces.

Also that king is said to have greatly respected his parents. Also when that king was ruling he sent out his personal slaves and put them at Panyula' and they were called the people of Panyula'. Then, the slaves who came into his possession while he was king, he put those at Lipenno. Then the people of Panyula' and the people of Lipenno rendered a tribute of fish. Also they paddled if ArumPone went sailing. Also they acted as bearers if ArumPone went travelling.

When 72 years of ruling were completed, he gathered together the people of Bone with the vassals, and ArumPone said, 'This is why, people, I have gathered you together. I am old, and I feel my body to be weak as well. But I want to see you on parade.'[31]

Following that, the people of Bone gave their assent and the people agreed too on a day. When the appointed day came, the people paraded, the Woromporong was unfurled. After the people had paraded, (ArumPone) received as guests the people of Bone with the vassals. After the people had eaten, ArumPone said, 'Just one thing more, people, I want to announce to you people of Bone. This, my child called Wé Benrigau' I wish to rule in Bone, if I die. To her hands also I entrust the treaty which Puatta Mulaiépanreng enjoined me (to hand on).'

Following that, the people went home. Only one night after he had made his will, illness struck him and he also departed (this life).

4

Our lord Kerrampélua' begat Mallajangngé riCina <She who disappeared in Cina>. When our lord Kerrampélua' had passed on, then Makkalempié ruled in Bone. That had been in the will of her parents, and, may my belly not swell, Wé Benrigau' was her personal name and Daéng Maroa her title. She was also called the queen of Majang, and only when she ruled was she called ArumPone. She was praised as having intelligence.

Two years afterwards she had her menarche and it was thought best by her parents that she marry Arung Kaju, called La Tenribali. They had nine children, but only two are entered in this work. As for their (other)

31 Literally, in a state of preparation (presumably for war).

seven children, they still remain in the records on strips (of palm leaf).[32] But those of their children in this work are, may my belly not swell, called my lord La Tenrisukki' and La Tenrigora.

Makkalempié ruled and sent the king of Katumpi', in Attassalo, called La Dati', to ask about buying the hill of Cina for 90 buffalo bulls, and it was sold. Our lady Makkalempié bought the hill south of Laliddong, and she bought it for 30 buffaloes. Following that, she ordered people to settle on the hill of Cina. She also ordered them to lay out gardens. She also ordered people to go to the hill south of Laliddong which she had bought.

Then two years after they had laid out gardens on the hill of Cina and they had worked up the fields south of Laliddong, the agriculture and the gardens of those who lived at Cina were destroyed by the people of Katumpi'. ArumPone gave orders that the king of Katumpi' should call the past to mind.[33]

Only three months after the message of ArumPone that the king of Katumpi' should call the past to mind had been sent, the official of ArumPone was killed. (Bone) attacked Katumpi', and Katumpi' was conquered by the people of Bone, it was plundered on that very day, and the fields east of Laliddong and north of Laliddong were taken.

Then the youngest son of ArumPone, called La Tenrigora, he was given his inheritance in Majang and in Cina. Thus La Tenrigora was called Arung Cina, he was also called Arung Majang.

Then the child of ArumPone called La Tenrisukki', may my belly not swell and may I not part (from life), to him the kingship of Bone was handed over. He was enthroned by his parents, and called ArumPone, may my belly not swell, whose named was La Tenrisukki'. He was 11 years (old)[34] when kingship was handed over to him by his parents.

Then after our lady Makkalempié had enthroned her child and established (him) in the royal hall, she just went to Cina to live with her youngest son, called La Tenrigora.

32 Compare this with the similar statement in Chapter 1 and the note there.
33 Presumably, he was being asked to remember that he had bought it on behalf of Bone.
34 Other versions of the chronicle say he was 19 years old.

Makkalempié lived in Cina for four years. Then it happened one day that Makkalempié chanced just to go up to her attic and thereupon sat down in the attic on part of a loom. Then there was what the men of old call Fire God. It just chanced to be there turning hither and thither at the house, it followed the staircase,[35] so the story goes. It came, so the story goes, up into the house turning hither and thither all the time, it even mounted up to the attic. Yet when the Fire God died out, then too Makkalempié was not to be seen. She was called Mallajangngé riCina.

5

Mallajangngé riCina begat Mappajungngé <He who uses an umbrella>. La Tenrisukki', may my belly not swell, ruled in Bone. It was already four years after rule had been handed over by his parent when she who disappeared passed on. Then he married his first cousin called Wé Tenrisongké. They were the parents of, may my belly not swell, he who was called La Ulio and entitled Boté'é <the Fat Man>.

All the kings of the hills together came to merge their land with Bone, and they were established as vassals.

Also when he ruled in Bone, it happened that the Datu of Luwu, entitled Dewaraja, attacked Bone. Then the Luwurese landed south of Cellu, and took up a position. Then afterwards there were skirmishes between the parties in the roads and part of the women escaped, and the people at Attassalo followed them. They went southwards towards Attassalo at the hour before dawn, when the Luwurese right there raised the war cry. (The Luwurese) wanted to follow up their cry. But also the people of Bone had settled into position at Biru. Just as the dawn of the day was breaking, the Luwurese spied (the people of Bone), then (the Luwurese) saw the women in the road east of Anrobiring. For these, (the Luwurese) charged ahead. The people of Attassalo struck at the Luwurese. The Luwurese were recognised by the people of Bone. The Luwurese were put to disorderly flight. The umbrella of the Datu of Luwu was captured. Yet the Datu of Luwu was not wounded. It just happened that ArumPone restrained the people, saying, 'Do not wound the person of the Datu of Luwu.'

35 That is, the staircase leading up from the ground into the house.

Then (the Datu of Luwu) was followed eastwards right up to his ship. There were only 20 reaching the ship of the Datu of Luwu. It was only a small ship that he got to and departed in. He sat in it and went to his territory. So from this, there was again an umbrella in Bone. It was actually a red umbrella, the umbrella of the Datu of Luwu that was captured. Hence La Tenrisukki', may my belly not swell, was entitled Mappajungngé.

Also when he was ruling in Bone, the people of Mampu and the people of Bone quarrelled. War broke out between them and they raised the war cry against each other, so that they clashed south of Itterrung. The people of Mampu were repulsed and made to go back to their territory. Then Arung Mampu went out and made obeisance, offering a thousandfold ransom.[36] 'You may do anything, ArumPone, if only you do not send away (from me) my child and my wife.'

ArumPone said, 'I only send you home, Arung Mampu, you establish yourself as a vassal of Bone, you are not unimportant in Bone, you do not lack pure gold, long cloths, long possessions, for you to hand on to your descendants.'

After that Arung Mampu was sworn (to loyalty). After Arung Mampu and his retinue were sworn (to loyalty), ArumPone returned to his territory.

When he had ruled 27 years, an illness struck him. He assembled the people of Bone, saying, 'My illness is serious, but if I die, there is my child, called La Ulio, he will succeed me.' After he had made his will, then too the way to his burial was clear.

6

Mappajungngé begat Matinroé rItterrung <He who sleeps in Itterrung>.[37] When Mappajungngé had passed on, Boté'é in turn ruled in Bone since that had been willed by his parent, and, may my belly not swell, La Ulio was his personal name.

36 Matthes (1874a: 692) explains that the phrase *sebbu kati* does not mean 1,000 *kati*, but 8,888 reals, 88 duits. The repetition of the eight applies in various levels for different offences. A *kati* is a unit of monetary value, but the word is probably also associated with an alternative (and perhaps older) meaning of gold.

37 This is the first occurrence of the normal form of high-status necronym referring to the place or some other circumstance of the individual's death.

It is said that while yet young, he was corpulent. His bearers were more than seven and his bearers were interchanging. Hence he was entitled Boté'é.

As king he went on inspections and gave orders (for improvement). Also he was said to like cockfighting, and was said to be well-balanced.

Then Boté'é is said to have married the child of the king of Pattiro, entitled Magadingngé <He who wears armbands>,[38] and she was called Wé Tenriwéa, and entitled Danraé.[39]

Boté'é married the child of Magadingngé, and they bore, may my belly not swell, (a child) called La Tenrirawé and entitled Bongkangngé;[40] they also bore, may my belly not swell, (a child) called La Icca'; they also bore, may my belly not swell, (a child) entitled Tenripauang; they also bore, may my belly not swell, (a child) called I Lémpe'.

This Boté'é as king was the first to be attended by Kajao Laliddong.[41] Also as king he made a treaty with the Karaeng of Gowa[42] called Daéng Matanré.[43] As well, the agreement is called Sitettongenna Sudeng La Téariduni <Sudang and La Téariduni standing together>.[44] Also he conquered the Datu of Luwu. When he stayed at Cénrana he was with the Karaeng called Daéng Bonto,[45] the child of Daéng Matanré. The Karaeng took the contents, ArumPone took the stalk.[46]

Boté'é was also married in Mampu to Wé Tenrigau', the child of Arung Mampu called Daéng Palimpu.

Also when Boté'é was ruling in Bone, the Karaeng of Gowa came here and was the first (Karaeng of Gowa) to set foot on the land of Bone. Then it is said the Karaeng of Gowa and ArumPone conferred south of

38 This sense of the title is somewhat uncertain. Another possibility is 'the man the colour of ivory'.

39 On one reading, this could be Daraé, which means 'the Blood', but it is probably better to read Danraé and relate it to the old Bugis word *denra*, meaning a high-status woman.

40 The literal meaning of this title is uncertain.

41 This name, which literally means 'the old man of Laliddong', refers to the best-known sage or legal authority in Bugis customary law.

42 Karaeng is a Makasar title and is always applied to the ruler of the State of Gowa.

43 This is Tumapa'risi' Kallonna.

44 These are both famous swords in the regalia of the two courts. For La Téariduni, see Bakkers (1866: 190, and Plate 1). Both items were removed to Batavia in the early twentieth century but were returned in the 1930s—La Téariduni to Watampone and Sudang to Sungguminasa, where they are still kept (Budiarti 2007).

45 This is Tunipalangga.

46 The word means, literally, the central rib of a leaf, such as a palm leaf. As Matthes has written in the manuscript, the sense means the ArumPone got the land and the Karaeng got what was in the land.

Laccokkong[47] on (the question of) the people of Gowa and the people of Bone killing each other. If a person of Bone struck the blow, the Karaeng of Gowa would wrap (the body) in a sarong, if a person of Gowa struck the blow, ArumPone would wrap (the body) in a sarong.[48] Also while he was ruling, the Karaeng of Gowa was accompanied (by him). They took the thousandfold ransom[49] from the people of Wajo at, so it is said, Topacceddo.[50]

When 25 years of ruling in Bone were completed, the people of Bone were gathered together, and he said, 'I want, people, to hand over the kingship to my child called La Tenrirawé.'

The people of Bone gave their assent, and his child was enthroned over seven days and seven nights. After his child was enthroned, our lord Boté'é went down from the palace. He divided his territory into two. There were those who went to Mampu to his wife, there were those who went to Bone.

Then Boté'é was angry with his nephew, called La Paunru. He was angry too with his first cousin who was king of Paccing and called La Mulia. They wanted to entrust themselves to the people of Mampu and that pardon be sought. Then it chanced that Boté'é went to spend the night (with his wife) in Mampu when the people of Mampu had not yet got the message to (him), and Boté'é went down to cockfight. He saw his first cousin and his nephew. All over again he was newly angry. When he left to return again to Bone, La Paunru and La Mulia consulted together, 'It is good that we follow up the old man. We will entrust ourselves (to him) and so at least we will ask for pardon.'

When he reached Itterrung, Boté'é turned to look back, and he saw his first cousin and his nephew, and he thought himself to be followed by them wanting to run amuck. He ordered his litter to be set down. So La Paunru felt himself to be deprived of his freedom and he just ran amuck slaying Boté'é and himself together. I La Mulia slew another person as well. Boté'é was called Matinroé rItterrung.

---

47 The name is known within the modern town of Watampone, but this seems an unlikely identification in the context.

48 The intention of these provisions was, presumably, to show their mutual respect and toleration.

49 See the note on the thousandfold ransom in the account of the previous reign.

50 Noorduyn (1955: 68) suggests this was in southern Wajo, on the Cenrana River.

7

Matinroé rItterrung begat Matinroé riGucinna <He who sleeps in his urn>. Then Bongkangngé ruled for he had already been made king in the lifetime of his parent, and, may my belly not swell, La Tenrirawé was the personal name of Bongkangngé. Bongkangngé was his title. He was married in Timurung to the queen of Timurung, called Tenripakkiu, and there were two children. One called La Maggalatung, he died young. One called Punna riSompa,[51] he was trained to succeed in Timurung, and died by a person running amuck. I Da Kalula was the name of the person who ran amuck.

Bongkangngé was, in fact, not known for being clever, yet he was praised as good-hearted, he was praised as a person who enjoyed entertainment, he was also praised as righteous, he was also praised as liberal-minded, he was also praised as a conqueror, he was also praised as liking duels to the death. He is also said to have liked family who were of lower status (than him), he is also said to have taken advice from his parents, but he is said to have been extremely angry if he were annoyed.

Also when he was ruling, he appointed people to act as officials and the officials were the heads of his nobility. (There was) a head for the territory, and for the young men of noble birth,[52] and for all who were designated craftsmen, and also for all those women who acted as companions,[53] for the bearers, for the wood-carriers, for the servants-in-waiting, for the (servants) who arranged the (court's) food, for the concubines.[54]

Also then there began to be guns.

When Bongkangngé was ruling, it happened that the Karaeng of Gowa entered Bone for cockfighting. Then a hundred *katis*[55] rested on the contest for the Karaeng, and ArumPone wagered the people of Panyula' with (its)

51 The meaning of this name seems to be the person to whom homage is paid, but there may be other possibilities.

52 Matthes (1872: Vol. 3, p. 69) has a note on the difficulty of translating the Bugis found in all of NBG 99, NBG 100 and NBG 101. We follow his general sense and look also to the equivalent *ana'bura'ne* in Makasar.

53 This phrase is obscure. It may mean they acted as wet nurses.

54 Matthes (1872: Vol. 3, p. 69) has a note on the difficulty of translating this. The translation as 'concubines' remains a guess.

55 A *kati* is here a unit of value. The phrase used does not necessarily mean exactly 100 of them. See Note 36.

territory. The cock of the Karaeng was red, the cock of ArumPone was white with red on wings and breast. The cock of the Karaeng was killed, and the hundred *katis* also paid out.

Also while he was ruling, the people to the west of the wood decided to attach themselves to Bone. He conquered Awo, Téko, and he also conquered them all at Attassalo, which was an enemy for the second time.

Also when he was king, there were the Three Powers[56] blocking the door to Gowa and they attached (themselves) to Bone and were established as vassals. Then the Karaeng entered (Bone) so that south of Méru the Makasars and the people of Bone clashed. They fought for seven days and after that the people conferred and the people of Bone and the people of Gowa were at peace with each other. They determined that the people of Bone went up to a boundary south of the River Tangka and running up to the high (country).

Also when Bongkangngé was ruling, the was a *datu*-ship[57] acknowledged by homage in Sawitto, and (the *datu*) was driven out and came here to Bone.

Also when he was ruling, the people of Soppeng divided (themselves) within the territory. Arung Soppéng-Riaja,[58] entitled Mabbélua'é <He with the hair (on his head)>, was deprived of power and came here to Bone. When Mabbélua'é was thus in Bone he married the sister, called Tenripauang, of the king of Bone. She bore (a child) called I Dangke' and entitled Lébaé <the Monarch>. (The child) was also called the Datu of Mario. The sister of ArumPone called, may my belly not swell, Wé Lémpe' married the *maddanreng*[59] called La Saliwu, and they were second cousins. They were the parents of, may my belly not swell, (a child) called La Tenrirua, whose name after death was Matinroé riBantaéng.

56 This is not the famous Tellumpoccoé or Three Power alliance of 1582, which is described below, but an earlier grouping of Bulo-Bulo, Lamatti and Raja—all south of Bone. In other sources, they are called Tellulimpoé or the Three Communities.

57 *Datu* is used as a term for the ruler in several states of the peninsula.

58 This means West Soppeng. It appears to be a mistake for Soppeng-Rilau or East Soppeng. This man is known in sources from Soppeng as La Makkarodda To Tenribali (Nur 2007: 61).

59 The *maddanreng* was one of the chief ministers of the court of Bone and was traditionally charged with business beyond the court. The name means, literally, 'He who is near (the ruler)'.

Also while Matinroé riGucinna[60] was ruling, it happened that the nephew of the Karaeng of Gowa, called Daéng Pabéta entered Bone. The nephew of the Karaeng was here in Bone and just afterwards met a person running amuck and was entitled by the people of Bone Daéng Patobo'.[61] Daéng Patobo' was in Bone, and it happened that the Karaeng called Daéng Bonto[62] attacked Bone, and thus they landed at Cellu. Then the people of Bone and the Makasars made war. Daéng Bonto was wounded with *ipo* poison.[63] The people fought for five days. Then the Karaeng went back to his territory.

Two years after they made war at Cellu, it happened again that the Karaeng of Gowa attacked Bone. Thus on a large river[64] (he) placed a fort and the people of Bone and the people of Gowa fought. Daéng Patobo' was wounded by a steel (lance). For more than seven days they fought. Then an illness struck the Karaeng and he had to return to his territory, and died within two months.

It happened again that the Karaeng Daéng Parukka[65] attacked Bone. All the people west of the forest became enemies. As for the people of Timurung, they deserted their children and their wives, and came here eastwards to Bone, crowding themselves in. Only women, so the story goes, were said to be living in Timurung, together with their children. As for the five territories to the east, they brought the wives up to Cinennung, and the men entered Bone, crowding themselves in.

Since the people of AwamPoné[66] were also enemies, the Karaeng placed a fort there at Pappolo. When his fort was finished, he advanced on Bone. He burnt half of Bukaka and Takké Ujung. When it was already afternoon, the Makasars wanted to drive away (the people), and they were recognised by the people of Bone. The Makasars were repulsed and the Karaeng was forced to flee as far as Cempaé, and the Makasars were almost all killed. The Karaeng was cut down. La Tunru' was the name of (the man) who cut him down.

60 The Bugis here and in the following section gives the name as Matinroé riGucié, or 'He who sleeps in an urn'. There is no significance in the variation.

61 This is a play on words. *Pabéta* means conqueror; *Patobo'* means a stabber (with a *kris*). This is the ruler of Gowa known as Tunijallo'.

62 That is, Tunipalangga.

63 There is a vast literature on the poison known as *ipo* or *upas*. For an introduction, see Yule and Burnell (1903: 952–9).

64 Probably the Walennae or the Great River that flows through the centre of the peninsula.

65 That is, Tunibatta.

66 That is, North Bone.

There was only the Karaeng called Daéng Padulung[67] and the people of Gowa looked (to him). The Karaeng of Tallo sent to Bone. The envoy of the Karaeng of Tallo announced, 'There were two lords of ours, one you have cut down on a mat,[68] and one you have cut down in the centre of the field. But we have wished for what is good, we have not wished for what is bad.'

Kajao Laliddong said, 'Since that is what you say, tomorrow I will go out to the Karaeng.'

It was early the next morning when Kajao Laliddong went out. Then the Karaeng made a treaty and afterwards they agreed on its terms. After the Karaeng of Tallo, called Daéng Padulung, had made a treaty with the people of Bone, Daéng Patobo' was made king in turn in Gowa.

Also when that Bongkangngé was ruling in Bone, he quarrelled with the Datu of Luwu, called Sangkaria. Since again the Luwurese were unwilling to acknowledge Cenrana as territory (of Bone), yet again the Luwurese attacked Cenrana. Thus there were two occasions when the land of Cenrana was captured by the people of Bone at the point of the sword. Then the people of Unyi began to be slaves to Bone.

Also when Bongkangngé was ruling in Bone, he made friends with the Arung Matoa of Wajo called To Uddama, and he also made friends with the king of Soppeng, entitled Pollipué.[69] When they were working together at Cenrana, they met to become brothers. Then they agreed to make each other brothers, saying, 'It is good to meet at Timurung and conclude our discussion when the moon is full.'

When the day that had been fixed came, they met in Timurung. There were all the people of Bone and their vassals, there were also all the people of Wajo and their vassals, and there were also all the people of Soppeng and their vassals. Then they placed a meeting house in Bone and then placed there a cockpit. When the new moon rose, the people of Bone, the people of Wajo and the people of Soppeng gathered together. ArumPone, the Arung Matoa of Wajo and the Datu of Soppeng sat down together and made those three lands brothers to each other. Indeed it also went as far as if they were brothers from the same mother and the same father, Bone the

67 That is, Tumenanga riMakkoayang of Tallo.

68 That is, by sickness.

69 In Soppeng sources, this is La Mappaleppe' Patola'é. See Nur (2007: 64–70).

eldest, Wajo was the child in the middle, Soppeng was the youngest. After that they took an oath together. They swore that they would not diminish each other, that they would not envy each other's pure gold, long cloths and fine possessions. After that they buried stones, and called the lands Tellumpoccoé <the Three Powers>.[70]

That king was greatly liked by the people of Bone, and greatly cherished. Two years after burying the stones for Tellumpoccoé, an illness struck Bongkangngé. He gathered the people of Bone together. 'This, people, I announce to you, there is my younger brother to succeed me.'

He summoned his younger brother, called, may my belly not swell, La Icca'. He said, 'This I announce to you, that I am ill. Take care of your affairs for I intend that you should rule here if I should die. This also I announce to you, that if I die, there are no restrictions on making my funeral. I intend you to marry your sister-in-law. May you indeed be lucky and may you have a child by Arung Timurung. I intend that you marry. It is hard to find a woman with such quality and intelligence as she has. May you care for the land of Bone.'

After he had made his will, he died. He was called Matinroé riGucinna.

8

Matinroé riGucinna was the brother of Matinroé riAddénénna <He who sleeps on his staircase>. When Matinroé riGucinna had passed on, may my belly not swell, then La Icca' was king in Bone since that was willed by his elder brother. After he had arranged the funeral of Matinroé riGucinna, he was enthroned.

After he was enthroned, he married the queen of Timurung, Tenripakkiu. They bore, may my belly not swell, (a child) called La Tenripale', entitled To Akkempéang. They also bore, may my belly not swell, Wé Tenrijello', and she was entitled Makkalaru'é, and also there was one who died while young.

70 This important treaty, which can be dated to 1582, was frequently appealed to over the following centuries. The burial of the three stones, after a ceremony involving the breaking of eggs, symbolises the permanency of the treaty. The symbolism is discussed by Matthes (van den Brink 1943: 548) and the political situation by Noorduyn (1955: 85–6), who also lists various copies of a text of the treaty (p. 27) in the manuscripts available to Matthes and published by him (Matthes 1864: 532–6). See also Nur (2007: 66–8).

When he who was called La Icca', may my belly not swell, was ruling in Bone, it happened that the Karaeng of Gowa attacked Bone. But he did not arrive and the Karaeng went back.

The thoughts of that king, may my belly not swell, are not known. Only the facts of what happened are entered in (this) work.

When he was ruling, the people of Bone began not to know how to discuss things with each other. He was angry at Arung Pallenna, called La Panaongi, and entitled To Pawawoi. Then (Arung Pallenna) was exiled as far as Sidenreng. When he was bored with staying in Sidenreng, he wanted only to come back to Bone and ask pardon. He was ordered to go away up to Buki'é. Arung Pallenna was followed and killed. The king of Paccing too was killed. The *maddanreng* of Palakka, called To Saliwu-Riwawo, was also killed. Many noblemen of Bone were killed too. (La Icca') plundered people who should not be plundered. He promoted people who should not be promoted. The inability of the people of Bone to discuss things with each other increased, but still nothing was done.

This is how, so the story goes, the break was made. It happened one day that there was a man of Bone and (La Icca') went to deprive him of his wife, and when he got there, the man wanted to kill him. The man fled, and then (La Icca') just killed the man's wife. After that he put (the house) to the torch and the fire consumed half of Bone up to Matajang and came to the west of Macégé'. The people of Bone scattered everywhere. Then what nobles there were took themselves off, and went south to Majang. Our lord of Majang said, 'Why are you here?'

The people of Bone said, 'We do not know how to tell of it, lord. Just look and you will see northwards the territory of Bone.'

When our lord of Majang looked, he struck his breast, and said, 'The change, the work of my lord (La Icca'), is distressing. But the people of Bone do not yet express our opinion. Send someone to get me my nephew called Da Malaka, from Mampu, for only he is an old nobleman.'[71]

The people said, 'He is just north in Palakka, lord.'

He was sent for and brought. Before long, he was there. Da Malaka said, 'Why, lord, have you sent to get me?'

71 Literally, an old ruler.

Our lord of Majang said, 'This is why you have come here. Do you not see the smoke and fire in Bone?'

Da Malaka said, 'It is clear, lord, I do see it.'

'That is why I sent to get you. What do you think about it?'

Da Malaka just remained silent. Yet three times the question was put by our lord of Majang, and after that (Da Malaka) said, 'I am afraid, lord, and it is as well if I am surrounded by no more than reproaches.'

Our lord of Majang said, 'We are both together in this. We share but one neck.'

Da Malaka said, 'Such is your word, lord, and there is no error (in it) which comes to mind. What you have expressed clears the honour of the land. Although our lords of former times have already made the land more honoured than their own persons, yet they have not laid down a customary procedure for driving out (a king). I, then, initiate this procedure. I will drive out my nephew.'

It happened that Da Malaka set up a statement. He sent (an envoy) to his nephew to say, 'Depart, you are not worthy of the land.'

The envoy arrived and there on the ground[72] (La Icca') met and received the person who had been sent. Yet even before he had delivered all (his message), the envoy was killed, and after that (La Icca') put to the torch all the houses of Bone within the wall.

When our lord of Majang was informed that there was no longer a house within the wall, our lord of Majang said, 'Carry me, fellows, and bring (me) to Bone, and I will go to slay myself and my grandson. It is possible for me to oppose and kill him and myself, since he is no king.'

Da Malaka said, 'I will also go, for by now the opinion is secure that we share but one neck.'

All the people went to Bone. (La Icca'), all by himself, came to meet them there. When he saw the common people, he rushed straight at them and killed many people. The affair was like this, so the story goes. There were those he rushed straight at, and they fled. There were those behind him,

72 That is, not in a formal audience in the palace.

and they pursued him, until he was exhausted. Then he went and leant on his staircase, and our lord of Majang split open the head of his grandson, and he died. Then he was called Matinroé riAddénénna. The people also say that he is the man who took his palace (with him). It was 11 years he ruled, and then he died.

9

Matinroé riAddénénna was first cousin to Matinroé riBettung <He who sleeps in Bettung>. After the death of Matinroé riAddénénna, the people of Bone gathered together with our lord of Majang and consulted together. 'Whoever will we set up as king?'

Then the king of Majang proposed a plan. The king of Majang said, 'The only person who is in the category for you to take as king is my grandson La Pattawe', the child of Arung Pallenna, and grandson of Makkalempié.'

So it came about that the people of Bone agreed to give their allegiance (to him) and to give their assent. Arung Kaju was then established as king in Bone, and was called ArumPone. He was called La Pattawe'. Then ArumPone married the queen of Mampu. Their child, may my belly not swell, was called Tenritappu.[73] Then La Tenrirua, may my belly not swell, married his first cousin called Dangke', and they were the parents of (a child), may my belly not swell, called La Tenrisui.[74] But no tale from the time of his kingship is now to be heard. They merely say that he ruled for only seven years in Bone. He went to Bulukumpa,[75] and there an illness struck him, and that also carried him off and he died.

10

Matinroé riBettung begat Matinroé riSidénréng <She who sleeps in Sidénréng>. Since she, called I Tenritappu, was the child of Matinroé riBettung, she was called ArumPone.

73 The name Wé Tenritappu also appears in many places as Wé Tenrituppu. Matthes (1872: Vol. 3, p. 73) is wrong in his note; she is not the same person as I Dangke'.

74 As correctly noted in Chapter 13, this was a daughter and her name was Wé Tenrisui.

75 The modern spelling is Bulukumba.

When she was ruling, she established Arung Pitu <Seven Arungs>.[76] The headman of Tibojong was called Arung Tibojong. The headman of Ta' was called Arung Ta'. The headman of Ujung was called Arung Ujung. The headman of Poncéng was called Arung Poncéng. The headman of Tanété was called Arung Tanété. The headman of Macégé' was called Arung Macégé'. ArumPone said, 'For this, people, I have established you as Arung Pitu, I want you to look after the agriculture and the guests of the queen of Bone, since I am a woman, and I want you to seek the scattered contents of the palace. But I establish you as Arung Pitu not so that you might tread on the edge of the land of Bone,[77] and not so that you might drive (people) to go away, and not so that you might bequeath things to your children without me knowing of it, unless, that is, we who are all descendants of Mappajungngé sit down together and agree together who is king (or queen) in Bone. Only after that go and after that also go forward with your bequests to your children and grandchildren.'

Also when she was ruling in Bone, it happened that the Karaeng of Gowa attacked in order to bring the Islamic faith, and he made Ajatappareng follow the war cry. Tellumpoccoé went to meet the Makasars. Hence the Karaeng went back to his own territory.

Only one year after, it happened that the Karaeng attacked Pandang-Pandang, and again Tellumpoccoé went and they met each other east of Bulu' Sitompo', and the people threatened each other and Tellumpoccoé was repulsed. They went each to their own territory and the Tellumpoccoé alliance of Bone, Wajo and Soppeng was destroyed.

One year after Tellumpoccoé was destroyed, it again happened that the Karaeng attacked Soppeng. Then the people of Bone and the people of Wajo did not go to help the people of Soppeng. Soppeng was conquered and the people of Soppeng became Muslim.

One year after the confession of faith by the people of Soppeng, it again happened that the Karaeng attacked Wajo. The people of Wajo submitted and the confession of faith was again introduced.

---

76 This name was used for the *Hadat* or Council of Bone in later times. In the list of members given by Bakkers (1866: 70–1) and as noted by Matthes (1872: Vol. 3, p. 74), Tanété is divided into north and south areas, each with its own *Arung*, thus making up seven *Arung* in all.

77 This might mean they were not to rock the land of Bone like a boat or bring it to destruction, as Matthes suggests (1872: Vol. 3, p. 74). Alternatively, it might mean they were not to go near, or across, the borders of the kingdom.

One year after the confession of faith by the people of Wajo, ArumPone went to Sidenreng wanting to inquire about the conditions of the Islamic faith. She arrived in Sidenreng and became Muslim. Also there in Sidenreng an illness struck her and carried her off. Nine years she ruled in Bone, then died, and was called Matinroé riSidénréng.

11

Matinroé riSidénréng was first cousin to Matinroé riBantaéng. When Matinroé riSidénréng passed on, the people of Bone gathered together. Then they agreed on Arung Palakka, and he was also king of Pattiro, since he was a grandson of Mappajungngé on both sides. Mappajungngé and Arung Palakka had an umbrella raised (over them). His personal name, may my belly not swell, was La Tenrirua. Also he himself was trusted by the people of Bone to do whatever he liked with the land of Bone.[78]

Yet even before he had been king for three months, it happened that the Karaeng attacked Bone in the war about Islam. The Makasars built a fort at Cellu, and also the Karaeng built a fort at Pallette. Islamic faith was displayed for the people of Bone.

ArumPone said, 'Since, people, you trust me to do what I like with the land of Bone, you raised the umbrella (over me). The Karaeng is displaying to us something good, and so it is good that we share the Islamic faith. For there was a former agreement of ours with the Karaeng that should one discover anything good and shining bright,[79] then one would show it. This Karaeng says, "I say it is good and shining bright for me (the Karaeng) to hold to the religion of the Prophet." Moreover the Karaeng says, "If you accept my instruction, we will both be great, just Gowa and Bone, and together equally we will serve the One God."' ArumPone also went on to say, 'If, friends, you do not accept the good instructions of the Karaeng, he is in earnest and we will be forced to acknowledge him and be slaves in his name.[80] If you accept the good instruction of the Karaeng, he will relieve us of instruction on another occasion in future. You think I am not willing to fight and be killed. Indeed after this I will fight if he reneges on his undertaking to me.'

78 Literally, to make it lie on its front or its back.

79 In what follows, this is used metaphorically to mean true belief. True light is a familiar metaphor.

80 That is, as well as being subject to him by reason of defeat.

The people of Bone were united in refusing to give assent to the Islamic faith.

ArumPone was silent since ArumPone felt that the people of Bone were moving in other directions. ArumPone just took himself and went to Pattiro. Only his personal staff followed him. When he came to Pattiro, he talked again with the people of Pattiro, yet again they did not want to follow the Islamic faith. Our lord was silent and went up to the palace and kept to himself. Only his personal associates went with him. His children and his wife, he forced them all up into the palace.

When ArumPone had been put aside and gone to Pattiro, the people of Bone gathered together. They agreed together that ArumPone should be driven out. The people of Bone sent (an envoy) to go to Pattiro, and To Alaung was the name of (the man) who was sent. When To Alaung arrived in Pattiro, he went up to the palace. He said, 'To Alaung, sir. This is what the common people of Bone have sent me (to say), sir. It is not that we do not want you, but you do not want us. An enemy has come upon your servants in Bone, and you have left them.'

Our lord said, 'O, To Alaung, I deny that I do not want the people of Bone, I only scoff at the people of Bone in that I show them what is good and shining bright. I really want to lead you to the light. You, people, do not want (to come). But you are fixed, friends, in your darkness of mind. Yet I go to the light which the One God makes to burn in the Prophet.'

After To Alaung spoke, he returned to Bone. Again the people of Bone agreed together and they made the Arung Timurung king in Bone, since he was a child of Matinroé riAddénénna. He was called, may my belly not swell, La Tenripale' as his personal name, To Akkempéang as his teknonym. When he had passed on, he was called Matinroé riTallo'. When he was king, he made the people of Bone fight in the war about Islam.

After his departure, To Alaung went to Bone, and our lord also sent (an envoy) to go to the Karaeng there at Palletté. When his envoy arrived at Palletté, the Karaeng also sent (an envoy) to go to Pattiro. Karaeng Pettung was sent. When Karaeng Pettung arrived at Pattiro, our lord was besieged by the people of Pattiro and the people of the hills. He went to meet them and ran amuck, and he repulsed all the hill (people) and the people of Pattiro and finished them off in the hills at Maroanging.

After that our lord crossed to Palletté to meet the Karaeng. Only Karaeng Pettung occupied Pattiro. When our lord reached the Karaeng, the Karaeng said, 'It is good, friend, that you come here. For I ask you where all your private property is. Although you are not king of Bone, you still have property. Although I acknowledge you own Bone, that has changed hands.'

Our lord said, 'My personal property consists of Palakka and Pattiro and AwamPoné. As for Mario-Riwawo, that is also the personal property of my wife.'

The Karaeng said, 'Make the confession of faith and on that day also the sum total of what you own accepts the confession of faith. Bone will not enslave you, Gowa will not enslave you.'

Our lord said, 'It is only about the confession of faith, Karaeng, that I have come here.'

After that then the Karaeng said, 'I know that you own Palletté. But my standard has been set up and I claim it as my property, but since Palletté is indeed my property, I give (it) to you.'

After that our lord was given by the Karaeng a velvet jacket braided with pure gold weighing 1 *kati*.

Our lord said, 'If, Karaeng, you give me (this) so that I will not accompany the people of Bone in opposing you, I do not want to take it.'

The Karaeng said, 'You know, father of my daughter-in-law, that it was the custom of the people of former times, if they met a member of their family, that there was also made as an expression of the meeting an exchange of one slice of areca nut and one leaf of *sirih*.'

Our lord said, 'I will own that (jacket), Karaeng, since such is your word.'

Following that then our lord and the Karaeng made an agreement. (There was) our lord Matinroé riBantaéng, the Karaeng of Gowa who introduced Islam and the Karaeng of Tallo who introduced Islam. This was their agreement. The Karaeng said, 'As we (all here) make witness before the One God, may there be no more of our family[81] to be king in

81 The first 'we' is inclusive in contrast to the 'our', which is exclusive and therefore refers to the families of the Karaéngs of Gowa and Tallo.

Gowa and in Tallo if you do not possess your property, if you are treated poorly by your fellow people. If there is any evil affecting you, open your door and I will come in to your evil.'

Matinroé riBantaéng also said, 'O, Karaeng, may my paddy sheaves not thresh properly, may my total (harvest) not be complete, may mice not be kept clear from my (storage) pile, if there is anything affecting the land of Gowa. Although I swim on only one trunk of bamboo, I will come to a crisis[82] and to your difficulty, Karaeng. This will apply to your descendants and also to my descendants, if only (your) word to us is not broken, to us who are little people.'

Such was the agreement of Matinroé riBantaéng and the Karaeng. After our lord and the Karaeng had made the treaty, they returned again to Pattiro. Five nights after the Karaeng and our lord Matinroé riBantaéng had made the treaty, they turned their attention to Bone and there was a war against Islam. The people of Bone rendered homage and were made to take the confession of faith, and the Karaeng returned to his territory.

As soon as the Karaeng had gone away, Matinroé riBantaéng was ordered to leave by the people of Bone. He went out to Makassar and was a pupil[83] to Dato' (ri)Bandang. Then Matinroé riBantaéng was given a foreign name[84] by Dato' (ri)Bandang and *Adam* was the foreign name of Matinroé riBantaéng. He stayed with Dato' (ri)Bandang for a long time. Then he was given the choice of where to live by the Karaeng and he chose to live at Bantaeng. Hence he was taken there, and Matinroé riBantaéng stayed there, and there he reached his span of years, and he was called Matinroé riBantaéng.

12

Matinroé riBantaéng was driven out and he was first cousin to Matinroé riTallo'. After Matinroé riBantaéng had been driven out, the people of Bone agreed to make Arung Timurung king, since he was the child of Matinroé riAddénénna by the queen of Timurung. Then there was ArumPone, may my belly not swell, called La Tenripale', To Akkempéang his title.

82 Literally, to a corner.
83 Literally, a child.
84 That is, in this context, a Muslim name.

When he was ruling, he made the people of Bone return to the war about Islam. Bone was burned and the people of Bone submitted, its thousandfold ransom was not taken, its fine was not demanded and it was not plundered either. The people of Bone rendered homage and were made to accept the confession of faith and that was the end of the matter, for they all settled down as vassals (to Gowa). After the people of Bone were made to accept the confession of faith, all the vassals (of Bone) were made to accept the confession of faith. When the Karaeng had again gone back to his territory, Arung Timurung ruled in Bone. He passed on and was called Matinroé riTallo'.

Matinroé riTallo' was one of two siblings. His younger sister was called, may my belly not swell, Wé Tenrijello', and she was entitled Makkalaru'é. Makkalaru'é married the king of Sumali, called La Pancai. They were the parents of (a child) who was called La Maddaremmeng, *Salih* was his foreign name. He was made king in Timurung. Then Pattiro was taken, and Makkalaru'é was also queen of Pattiro. One of the other younger brothers of La Maddaremmeng, may my belly not swell, was called Tenriampareng. He was king of Cellu. One of the other younger brothers was called La Tenriaji, To Senrima was his teknonym. He was made king in AwamPoné. He also was called Pawélaié riSiang <He who passed away in Siang>.

She who was called, may my belly not swell, Wé Tenrisui married La Pottobune', the king of Tana-Tengnga. They were the parents of (a child) who was called Da Unru', may my belly not swell, (and one) who was called La Tenritatta, To Unru' being his teknonym, and who had no children, and (one) Da Tenrigerra, who also died without family, and (one) Da Ompo', who had no children, and (one) Da Éba, and (one) who was called, may my belly not swell, Wé Pappolobonga, Da Umpi being her teknonym. She was called Maddanrengngé <the Maddanreng>.

One year after the people of Bone made the confession of faith, (ArumPone) went out to Makassar and met Dato' riBandang and he was called Abdullah, as the foreign name of ArumPone. As king he was good-hearted. He was also said to be a person who enjoyed entertainment, he was also said to have been very interested in agriculture.

He married the child of Matinroé riSidénréng who was entitled Kaunangngé. Their child was entitled Dabe'. Dabe' was the bride of the child of the Karaeng of Gowa, who introduced Islam. Daéng Mattola was the name of the Karaeng's child who took Dabe' as a bride. Yet before her menarche, she died. It happened that ArumPone had no more children of equivalent status.

As king he went and returned from the Karaeng and it was a very long interval if there were three years between visits.

(Once) when it was time for him to visit Makassar, he arrived to visit Makassar. There illness struck him and illness carried him off. Since there in Tallo he is buried, he was called Matinroé riTallo'. There were 20 years of rule and he passed away.

13

Matinroé riTallo' had as his sister's child, Matinroé riBukaka. When Matinroé riTallo' passed on, his sister's child succeeded to rule in Bone, since that had been bequeathed (to him). La Maddaremmeng, may my belly not swell, was his personal name, *Salih* his foreign name. When he passed on, he was called Matinroé riBukaka.

When he was ruling, he made a white umbrella.

He married in Wajo Hatija, Da Senrima was her teknonym, the child of the Arung Matoa of Wajo, who was entitled To Ala'é. ArumPone had just one child, who was called Pakkoko'é, To Akkonéng his title.

Also when he was ruling, he extended the wall of Bone, extending it to the east and extending it to the south.

He was also said to be firm in practising religion. Also he cared strongly about it and was angry at those who did not care strongly about it. He ordered his parent to care strongly about it, but Makkalaru'é replied and said, 'I am not able (to do it), do not give (me) orders.'

He was angry at his parent and attacked Pattiro and sacked it. Makkalaru'é fled away to the Karaeng. The Karaeng of Gowa ordered ArumPone to be mindful. Bone was attacked by the Karaeng, and was conquered. ArumPone fled up to Cempu, he was followed, imprisoned, and carried away to Makassar. He was put in Siang.

Fifteen years he was king, and the people of Bone fled.[85] When he passed on he was called Matinroé riBukaka.

*

When Bone was deserted by Matinroé riBukaka, the brother of Matinroé riBukaka who was called To Senrima still remained in Bone. Yet again for another time Bone was attacked by the Karaeng and conquered, and prisoners were taken. That was called the Pasémpe' defeat, since the people of Bone went up to Pasémpe' to fight. To Senrima was also carried away and there he died. Then he was called Pawélaié riSiang.

Matinroé riBukaka just stayed in Siang together with the people of Bone who had been taken prisoner. That is the limit of what is told of Matinroé riBukaka though more is told in the place where he was living, but he was no longer king of Bone.

*

It reached the stage when there was only an official, whom the Karaeng set up to live in Bone. To Bala was the name of the person who acted as official in Bone. Then it was clear that the people in Bone had become slaves to the Makasars.

After 17 years of To Bala being the official, he supported the people of Bone (in revolt) and again the people of Bone were conquered by the Makasars, and To Bala was struck down. This was pronounced the To Bala defeat.

85 Presumably, this refers to the defeat at the hands of Gowa. The text is clear enough, but it is tempting to suggest an emendation to the effect that it was the ArumPone who fled.

The Matinroé riBontoala' crossed to Butung. This is said to have ended the enslavement of the land of Bone by the Makasars.

When To Bala died, Arung Amali in turn became official in Bone. After seven years of Arung Amali, he took the people of Bone off to Butung. There on Butung were the people of Bone, and there also was Matinroé riBontoala' together with the Dutch. Then the people of Bone were captured by Matinroé riBontoala', and Karaeng Bontomarannu and all the Makasars were captured as well, everything that there was on Butung.

The end.

The Bugis Chronicle of Bone: Bugis text

1

[p. 1][1]

Ianaé sure' poada-adaéngngi| tanaé riBoné| enrengngé mangkau' riBoné| angkanna rirapié méngkalinga| napauwé tomatowaé|

Tania upomabusung| tania upomawedda-wedda| tekkumatula poada| aseng tolébba| nasekko' rumasa sélo-sélo| ana' tolebbi'| Aga uwasimammémeng| kuinappa lakke'-lakke'| wija senrima mangkau'|

Ia garé' puttana arung ménré'é| riGaligo| dé'na riaseng arung| Aga tennassiseng tauwé| siéwa ada| Sianré-balémani tauwé| Siabelli-belliang| Dé'na ade'|apa'gisia riasengngé bicara| Riasengngi pitu-tturenni| ittana| dé' arung| Sikuwa toniro| ittana| tauwé tessise-ssiéwa ada| tekké ade'| tekké bicara|

Naiamani ammulanna| nangka arung| Engka séuwa esso| nasianré billa'é| letté| <m>péwattoni tanaé| Riasengngi| engkai sipasa makkua| Naia pajana billa'é| letté| <m>péwang tanaé| takko' engka tau rita| woroané| ritengngana padangngé| masangi<m>puté| Jajini sipulung tauwé| tassséwanua| tasséwanua| Iana riassiturusi| ritau maégaé| masengngéngngi| tomanurung|

Jajini passéuwa tangnga'| tau maégaé| Naia nassiturusi| <m>pokke'éngngi aléna| llao ritauwéro| nasengngé tomanurung| Lattu'i koria| Makkedani tau tebbe'é| "Iana mai kilaowang riko| Lamarupe'| amaséannakkeng| aja'na

1 Page numbers refer to the original manuscript, NBG 101.

muallajang| Mutudanna ritanamu| Naikona poatakkeng| Élo'mu élo' rikkeng| Napassuromuna kipogau'| Namau anammeng| na patarommeng| mutéaiwi| kitéaitoisi| Rékkua monromuno mai| naiko kipopuang|"

Puraikua| makkedaniro| riasengngé| tomanurung| "Madécénnami| Naianasia| upoadadako| temmakulléa' arung| apa' atawa'sia| Naé'rékkua maéloko| makképuang| engkaro puakku'| Iaro mupopuang| rékkua maélo'kkeng|"

Makkedani tomaégaé| "Mappékkoni kisseng| kipopuang| tekkitaé|"

Makkedani riasengngé| tomanurung| "Rékkuwa maélo' tonge-ttongekko| upaitaio|"

Makkedani tomaégaé| "Maélo' wégang nakkeng naé tabbuluko mamasé| lalengeng nakkeng|"

Puraikua| rilalengnganni tau maégaé| llao riasengngé riMatajang| Sianréni paimeng letté| wéro'é|

[p. 2]

Aga lettu'i riMatajang| napolé itani| tomanurungngé| tudang ribatu lappaé| Sangi<n>ridi eppa situdangeng| Watanna arungngé| séuwa pajungiwi| pajung maridi| séuwa pa<m>piriwi| séuwa tiwirangngi| salénranna|

Apa' llaoni kuria| ritomanurungngé| Makkedani Tomanurungngé| "Engkao Matoa|"

Makkedai Matowaé| "Io Puang|"

Inappani naisseng tomaégaé| makkedaé matoamua palé'| tasengngé arung| Makkedani to riasengngé manurung| "Iasiaro puakku'|"

Purai kua llaoni| tau maégaé| ritomanurung sangi<n>ridié| Nakkedana tau maégaé| "Iana mai kilaowang ridi' Puang| maélokkeng tamaséang|tamaradde'na mai ritanata'| Aja'na tallajang| Idi'na kipopuang| Élo'mu élo' rikkeng|passuromua| kua| Namauna <a>nammeng| enrengngé pattarommeng| mutéaiwi| kitéaitoisi| rékkuwa tudammuni' mai| Naikona poatakkeng| Mudongiri temmatipakkeng|"

Makkedai Tomanurungngé| "Teddua nawa-nawao| temma'balléccoko|"

Purai kua sikadonni| adanna tomanurungngé| tau maégaé| Rilékke'ni| Manurungngé| llao polé| riBoné| Ianaé Manurungngé| mangkau' riBoné| Ripatettongang langkana| Tépui langkanaé ripaté'ni Manurungngé| ttudang rilangkanaé|

Naia Manurungngéwé| tettadapi' méngkalinga| aseng rialéna| Gau'namenna ritellakangngi| Rékkua naitai lompo'é| napenno tau| natiroi naissemmenni ballalo| makkedaé| sikuwa tauro| makkedaé sikuwaro tau[2]| Aga naiamenna ritellarangngi| tania kupomabusung| Matasélompo'é[3]|

Matasilompo'éna | ma'bawiné riToro'| siala Manurungngé riToro'| tania kupomabusung| Nana' La Ummasa'| tania kupomabusung| enrengngé riasengngé| tania kupomatula| La Pattanrawanua| asenna| Limai sijajing| Naia saisa'é| koi mmonro riattoriolong rilullungngé| Ia muasi naripau risure'éwé| allapi-lapirenna| gau'é| riBoné| tassilapi-tassilapi|

Naia gau'na Manurungngé| Mangkau'é riBoné| iana mula patettong| riasengngé| Mappololéténg| Iana ppadengngiwi| assisulu'-sulurenna| akkéanungngé wali-wali tomakkéanué| Pada maradde' manenni ritauwé| Takkalaé mattiwi| tenriolanna siabbicarang| Iatona patettong Rapang Bicara| enrengngia Ade'| Naiana| riolai| Iatona Manurungngéwé| punna Baté Woro<m>porongngé|

Naia genne'-

[p. 3]

-na| patappariama| mangkau' riBoné| napasipulunni toBoné| Mapparénnaiwi| nakkeda "Tudanno m<a>i| Aja' mumarullé| Ianaritu ana'ku| riasengngé La Ummasa'| Iana ttolawa'| Iatona upattenning akkuluadangetta'|"

Puraikua billa'ni| letténi| Takko' dé'ni rita| ritudangenna| Manurungngé| ia dua mallaibini| laona[4] ritai| Paju<n>ridié| Dé'toni rita rionronna| Salénrangngé dé'toni| Ripatetto-mmutoni ballalo| mangkau'| tania kupomabusung| riasenna Puakku'| La Ummasa'| Nadé'tona pajung riBoné|

2 The close repetition of this phrase is a scribal error. In the manuscript, the second version of the phrase has been crossed through. Matthes also notes the readings of NBG 100 and NBG 99 to explain the passage.

3 *Sélompo'é*. The usual spelling is *Silompo'é*, as follows immediately.

4 The first *aksara* of *laona* is illegible, but this reading is supported by other manuscripts.

2

Manurungngé riMatajang poana'i| La Ummasa'| riasettoi To Mulaiépanreng| Naia mallajannana Puatta'| ia dua mallaibini| tania kupomabusung| La Umasa'na| mangkau' riBoné| Pawélaimani| nariaseng To Mulaiépanreng| Iana mangkau'| kalio'namani| ricinaongangngi| Rékkua engka nalaowi mappeddi'-essomani| Dé'nana pajung riBoné| Iatona riaseng| Panrébessié| Ripujito mainge'| Riasettoi maléleng| Riasettoi matanang|

Nallakkaina| ana'daranna Aru<m>Poné| riasengngé| Pattanrawanua| siala makkarungngé riPalakka| riasengngé| La Pattikeng|

Iatonaé mangkau' riBoné| nabétai Biru| nabétai Cellu| nabétai Malloi' nabétai| Anrobiring| nabétai Majang| Iatona sisala| ipa'na| makkarungngé riPalakka| riasengngé La Pattikeng| Nasiwangungang musu' maripa'| Natellumpuleng mammusu'| tessicau'| nasiajje'| mennang| Iatonaé| dé'pakua riaseng| rajanna riBoné| tanréna uwatanna|

Nadé' ane'na pattola| To Suallé mua napoana'| enrengngé| To Salawaka| naé pa'banua mua inanna| Aga naissengngi| mattampu' ana'daranna| mallakkaié riPalakka| Nalao ti<n>roini| riaseng| ripaitaianni| inappani massau ininnawana| Apa' naissenni| manguriwe'| ana'daranna| mallakkaié riPalakka| nata<m>paini toSuallé| enrengngé toSalawaka| Nakkeda "Lao sao urai' masiga'| riPalakka| apa' riasengngi manguriwe'na| anri'ku'| Naé' rékkua| alepperrenni| anri'ku'| pariappoppa-mmuani| raraé| mutampui| muwawai llao mai alau| masiga'| Kuapi mai risappe' lolona| kuatopi mai| ribissai|"

Madàka-rakatonisia| To Suallé| To Salawaka| llokka masiga'| Lattu'i riPalakka| matou'-tou'ni té' masiga'| risalassa'é| Tettuda-

[p. 4]

-ttopa| To Suwallé| To Salawaka| Nalepperenna makkunrainna| Arungngé riPalakka| Woroané ana'na| Manganro-manai'-maneng gemme'na| Mattou'-tou'menni To Suallé napariapoppangngi| raraé| nata<m>pui| risa<m>pu reppung| Nalaowangngi| alau riBoné| Naé' dé'i arungngé riPalakka| nariala ana'na|

Apa’ lettu’i riBoné| ripattou’-tou’ni té’ rilangkanaé| Inappani risappe’ lolona| inappato ribissai Ana’darannana Aru<m>Poné| riasengngé I Samateppa| risuro matuwoi| I Samateppana maruppengi| anauréna| Riobbira-mmémenni ritoBoné| wenni séwenni| makkedaé “Sipulukko baja| ttiwi’ paréwa musumu|”

Papai bajaé| engka manenni toBoné| sakke’ paréwa musu’| Ripadau’ni| Woro<m>porongngé| No’ni Aru<m>Poné| ribarugaé| Makkedai| Aru<m>Poné| “Ia mennang kupasipulungakko| to Boné| La Saliwuro asenna ana’ku’| Kerra<m>pélua’ pattellarenna| Upaléssoriniro akkarungengngé riBoné| Iatonaro ana’ku’| kupatenning uluadaé| napawarekkengiéngnga’ Puwatta’| nainappa mallajang|”

Sama kadoni to Boné| ia maneng| nainappana mangngaru| Nassuro mutona té’nai bissué| Naripatettong ballalo| pabbinru’é esso sésso| Narilanti’na Puatta’| Kerra<m>pélua’| riamauréna| pitungngesso| pitu<m>penni| Naiamanisi| garé’ taué| riwaéngngi raraé iana riaddojang| pitungngesso| pitu<m>penni| Apa’ genne’ni pakkawarué| inappani riwélésu lolona| Purai riwélésu érunna| no’ni risalassaé| Puatta’ Matowaé|

Puatta’ Kerra<m>pélua’| riaseng Aru<m>Poné| Iana mmonro rilangkanaé| Inaurénana| riasengngé| I Samateppa| tomatowaiwi| Naia Puatta’ Matowaé| rékkua engkana maélo’| llaowi| massuroni manai’ riana’na| makkedaé| “Té’sao manai| ripuammu| Muakkeda engka maélo’ nalaowi Puatta’| Assurosao <m>pawai|”

Iatonasia garé’ riwaéngngi raraé| makkeda “Laosaoromi muta<m>paiwi| tau nalaosa ttiwi’i Puatta’|” Makkuaniro garé’ gau’na Puatta’| rékkua engka nalaowi| namunagi-namunagi| gau’na Puatta’ Matowaé|

Naseppulo pitu taunna| napaléssori akkarungeng| anauréna| nateppani lasa maserro| Puatta’ Matowaé naiana mpawai| Nariasessi Puatta’| Mulaiépanreng|

3

Puatta' Mulaiépanreng| poanauréi Puatta' Kerra<m>péluwa'| Puatta'na Kerrampéluwa'| Mangkau' riBoné| Makkaru-mmémenni rituo-

[p. 5]

-na amauréna| apa' séwennimua| jajinna| naripaléssori akkarungeng riBoné| rijajinna| Rilanti' matoni| na To Sualléna mmawingi| na To Salawakana Makkedantana| Naé' rékkuwa| engka bicara namaterre'| napettui Tomabbicaraé| ripaté'ni manai' rilangkanaé| nakuwana sipakkeda| Na To Suwallénna <n>riwai raraé| nasipakkedana tauwé| wali-wali| Na To Salawakana sauriwi adaé| wali -wali|Naiyatona riwaéngngi raraé|iyana pannessai|asalanna tauwé|tau salaé| Riasettonisia| Pettu Bicaranna| Raraé|

Apa' marajani| Kerra<m>pélua'| tappini makkunrai| Inappani llao riPalakka| sita ncajiangngéngngi| Inappaniro sita| apa' lettu'i riPalakka| ritoanani rincajiangngéngngi| Narimanarinna| Naiatonaro| narimanarenna pasaé riPalakka| Nariwawana pasaé riPalakka llao riBoné| Nakuwa tauwé| riBoné mappasa|

Iatonaro llaona riPalakka rincajiangngéngngi|naripabbawinéna| siala sapposisenna| riasengngé| Wé Tenriroppo| ana' pattolana Arungngé riPaccing| Ia poana'i| tania kupomabusung| riasengngé| Wé Be<n>rigau'| Daéng Maroa pattellarenna| Iamuto riaseng Makkale<m>pié| Riasettoi Bissu riLale<m>pili'| Iana ripakkarung riMajang| Nariséséng| toBukakaé| saisa'| nariwawa riMajang| mmonro| Naiatonasia| napotauto Makkale<m>pié| Naripatettongina Saolampé'| riBoné|nariaseng Lawélareng| Napoasettoni Makkale<m>pié Puwatta' riLawélareng|

Naia Puatta' Kerra<m>péluwa'| ripuji malessi|Ripujitoi maléleng| Ripujitoi mapato lao<n>ruma| Ripujitoi malabo| Tenriase<m>pégasa tomacca| Dé' cau'i awaraningenna| Mau garé' inappa jajinna dé' mémessa napoléiwi takkini'| lettu' rimatoana| Tennaisseng mémessa riaseng| péneddingenna riasengngé takkini'| Aga naia poasengngi| Passoddo' Wakkaé|

Iatona arung mmula massuro poada| ada-passokkang ribalié| rékkua maélo'i mosengiwi balié| Apa' ia riasengngé tuppu-batu| enrengngiya timu-timu napogau' mémessa| arung rioloé| ménré'é riGaligo enrengngé massuroé|

Ianaé Kerra<m>pélua'| makkarung nawinru' baté Cella' dua| Naia Cella'é| dua Woromporongngé| séuwa ri<a>béona| séuwa riataunna| Natawa telluni toBoné aléna| Sétawang maccinaongiwi Cella'é| sitawang maccinaongiwi Woromporongngé| Naia Woromporongngé maccinaongiéngngi| toMajangngéna| enrengngé toMata-Angingngé| enrengngé toBukaka-Tengngaé| enrengngé toKawerrangngé| enrengngé toPalléngorengngé| enrengngé to

[p. 6]

-Mallarié| Namatowaéna riMatajang <m>pawai| Naia maccinaongiéngngi Cella'é| Riataunna| Woromporongngé| toPaccingngé| enrengngé toTanété| enrengngé toLémo-Lémoé| enrengngé toMasallé| enrengngé toMacégéé| enrengngé toBélawaé| naKajao Ciunna mpawai| Naia maccinaongiéngngi Cella'é| Ri<a>béona Woromporongngé| toArasengngé| enrengngé toUjungngé| enrengngé toPoncéngngé| enrengngé toTa'é| enrengngé toKatumpi'é| enrengngé toPadaccengngaé| enrengngé toMadello'é| naKajao Arasenna mpawai| Naia watanna ArumPoné| lélé uléni Aru<m>Poné| mappattuju|

Puatta' Kerra<m>pélua'| bbétai Palléngoreng| Sinri| Anrobiring| Iatona bbétai Lé<m>pang| Mellé| Iatona bbétai Sancénreng| Cirowali| Apala| Bakke'| Tanété| Attassalo| Soga| Lampoko| Lémoape'| Bulu'-Riattassalo| Parippung| Lompu|

Iatona mangkau'| napattau-séuwai| toBoné| na toPalakkaé| Ana'ni tanaé riPalakka| riBoné| Nangkana mmutama riBoné| Lima<m>panuaé|-Rilauale'| maddaoangngi tanana riBoné| Nangkatona Arungngé riBabauwaé| riasengngé La Tenriwasu| sita ménéttu-eppona| napaddaowi tanana| Napattau-séuwani ArumPoné| toBoné toBabauwaé| Ana'ni tanaé riBabauwaé riBoné| Nangkasi mutama arungngé riBarebbo| paddaowi tanana riBoné| Ana'ni tanaé riBarebbo| riBoné| Nangkatona muttama' Arungngé riPattiro riasengngé La Pauworong| sita Aru<m>Poné| apa' sipoipai| paddaowi tanana| Naripatuda-ppalilina| tanaé riPattiro| riBoné| Nangkatona muttama Cinennung| Ureng| Pasé<m>pe'| maddaowangngi tanana| Naripatudanna Tellu<m>panuwaé|

Éngkatoni arungngé riKaju riasengngé La Tenribali| paddaowi tanana riBoné| naripatudappalili'na Kaju| Nawata'-mutona duta| Arungngé riKaju| riana'na ArumPoné| ritellaé Makkalempié| tania kupomabusung| Wé Be<n>rigau' aseng <n>rialéna| Naritangke'na Arungngé riKaju| riArumPoné| Nainappana ppenning riwanuwanna| Arungngé riKaju|

Nakuwananaro mai riwanuwanna| nainappana lao botting| riBoné| Nallaibiningenna ArukKaju| riasengngé La Tenribali| ana'na Aru<m>Poné| ritella'é Makkalempié|

Nangkatona ArupPonré| maddaoangngi tanana riBoné| Nangka manettona mmuttama| Asérae Baté| riAttangngale'| enrengngé Asérae Baté| riAwangngale'| maddaoangngi tanana riBoné| Ana'ni riBoné Asérae Baté| riAttangngale'| Asérae Baté riAwangngale'|

Kerrampélua'na Mangkau' riBoné| nabéta maggulilingngi wanuwaé riBoné|

[p. 7]

Iatona arung riaseng| maserro pakarajai tomatoanna| Iatona Arung Mangkau'| napassu'i ata rialéna| nataroi riPanyula' | nariasenna toPanyula'é| Naia ata nalollongngé| angka makkarunna| kui nataro riLipenno| Na toPanyula'éna| silaong toLimpennoé| makkasiwiangang balé| Iatona mpisé rékkuwa llao mallopiwi ArumPoné| Iatona pampulé| rékkuwa llao mabélai ArumPoné|

Naia genne'na pituppulo duwa taunna| mangkau'| napasipulunni toBoné| séllili| Nakkedana ArumPoné| "Ia mennang kupasipulungakko| matowana'| usedditoni aléu' madodong| Naé' maéloka' mmitao maréwangeng|"

Puraikuwa| samakadoni toBoné| Massa<ppa>matoni tauwé| esso| Narapini| esso rita<n>raé| maréwangenni tauwé| Ripadau'ni Woro<m>porongngé| Purai maréwangeng tauwé| natowanani toBoné| séllili'| Purai manré tauwé| makkedani ArumPoné| "Iatopa mennang uwakkatta poadakko| toBoné| Iatu ana'ku' riasengngé Wé Be<n>rigau'| uwélorang makkarung riBoné| rékkuwa matéa'| Iatonaritu kupawarekkengi uluada| napatiangngéngnga' Puatta'| Mulaiépanreng|

Purai kuwa ssoro'ni tauwé| Naséwennimua purana mappaseng| nateppani lasa| nasia'mutona

4

Puatta' Kerrampéluwa'| napoana'ni Mallajangngé riCanai[5]| Ia pawélainna Puatta' Kerrampéluwa'| Makkalempiéna Mangkau' riBoné| Ia riappasengngang rincajiangngéngngi| tania kupomabusung| Wé Be<n>rigau' aseng rialéna| Daéng Maroa pattellarenna| Riasettoi Arungngé riMajang| mangkau'mani nariaseng ArumPoné| Ripuji kénawa-nawa|

Inappani duwa-ttaung| nawette' rara| Naripatangngarinna rincajiangngéngngi| Iana siala ArukKaju| riasengngé La Tenribali| Asera ana'nana| naé' duwamui ripauttama' risure'éwé| Naia ana'na pitué| kuisia mmonro riattoriolong rijori'é| Naia engkaé risure'éwé| tania kupomabusung| riasenna Puakku'| La Tenrisukki' enrengngé La Tenrigora| ana'naé[6]

Makkale<m>pié| mangkau'| nasuroi Arungngé riKatu<m>pi| riAttassalo| riasengngé La Dati'| mmélLau' mmelliwi bulu'é riCina| Aséra pulona tédong tenrilase'| Naripabbellinna| Nangellina| Puatta' Makkale<m>pié| Bulu'é riajanna Laliddong| Tellu-ppulo tédong naelliangngi| Puraikuwa| nassurona mmonroiwi Bulu'é riCina| Nassurotona palla'i| Nassurotona llaoiwi Bulu'é riajanna Laliddong| naellié|

Naduwa-ttaunna| napalla' Bulu'é riCina| enrengngé nauma| galungngé riajanna Laliddong| nariakkecca'

[p. 8]

-na pallao<n>rumana| enrengngé palla'na| mmonroé riCina| ritoKatum<m>pié| Massuroni ArumPoné painge'i| Arungngé riKatu<m>pi|

Natellu<m>pulemmua poléna surona| ArumPoné painge'i La Tu<m>pi[7]| nariwunona Jennanna ArumPoné| Natérini Katu<m>pi| Naribétana Katumpi' ritoBoné| Rirappa esso sésso| Narialana galungngé rilauna Laliddong| Enrengngé riawanna Laliddong|

5 The manuscript reads *Canai*, but as Matthes has written above it, the correct reading is certainly *Cina*.

6 *ana'naé*. There is a *pallawa* before this word, but none after it. Matthes has written in, and clearly prefers, the reading of NBG 99, *ianaé*, which then forms the first word of the next paragraph.

7 *La Tumpi* here means the ruler of Katumpi'.

Naia panyu<m>parenna ArumPoné riasengngé La Tenrigora| iana rimanariang riMajang| enrengngé riCina| Iana riaseng La Tenrigora| ArucCina| riasettoi ArumMajang|

Naia ana'na Aru<m>Poné| tania upomabusung| enrengngé upomatula| riasengngé La Tenrisukki'| Iana ripaléssori akkarungengngé riBoné| Narilanti'na rincajiangngéngngi| Nariasenna Aru<m>Poné| tania upomabusung| riasenna La Tenrisukki'| Seppuloi-sétaung naripaléssori akkarungeng rincajiangngéngngi|

Naia purana Puatta' Makkale<m>pi'é| nalanti'ni ana'na| napatudanni rilangkanaé| Nalaonasa riCina| mmonro silaong ana' panyomparenna| riasengngé La Tenrigora|

Napata-ttaung mmonro riCina| Makkale<m>pi'é Nangka séuwa esso| natakkau' ménré'mua Makkale<m>pi'é| riarakéanna| Nakuwana riarakkéangngé| tudangngi jarasana| Naé' engka naseng torioloé| Api Déwata| Natakko' <e>ngkamuaro mai| ma'balute' ribolaé| addénémmua garé' naola| Lattu'i garé' manai' ribolaé| ma'balute' ulé|Té'si manai riarakkéanna| Peddénisia <A>pi Déwataé| dé'tonisia rita Makkalempi'é| Riasenni Mallajangngé riCina|

5

Mallajangngé riCina| poana'i ritellaé Mappajungngé| tania kupomabusung| La Tenrisukki' Mangkau' riBoné| Pata-ttau-mmémenni purana ripaléssori angkaukeng| rincajiangngéngngi| napawélai Mallajangngé| Nasialana sapposisenna| riasengngé Wé Tenriso<ng>ké| Naiasi ncajiangngi tania upomabusung| riasengngé La Wulio| ritella'é Boto'é[8]|

Naengka manenna Arung Sébulu'é| mmuttama' riBoné| maddaoangngi tanana| Ripatuda-ppalilina|

Iatona Mangkau' riBoné| naengka Datué riLuwu| ritellaé Déwaraja| ttériwi Boné| Nakuwa| riattanna Cellu| ssoré Luwué| Nakuana ttaro tudang| Naia purana| sisokkang rilalengngé lluanni| makku<n>raié saisa' na toriAttassaloé tti<n>rosiwi| massu maniang riAttassalo| ridenniarié|

8 The name is given here, and on p. 9, ll. 21 and 22, as Boto'é. This is clearly a mistake for Boté'é, meaning 'the Fat Man', which occurs frequently below and is specifically justified in the text.

mmose-ttonisia-romai| luwué| Maélo'ni naoloi| osonna| Kkotonisia toBoné| riBiru| paranrung ttudang| Namappappana bajaé| makkarimatani luwué| naitani

[p. 9]

makku<n>raié| rilauna A<n>robiring| rilalengngé| Ianakkajuru'-juru'ki| Mattebbanni toriAttassaloé| luwué| Riarupai| luwué ritoBoné| Ripalari salani| luwué| Rialani pajunna Datué riLuwu| Iamua tennariwetta| Datué riLuwu| Engkanamua Aru<m>Poné| paleppengngi taué| nakkeda| "Aja' muwettai| watanna Datué riLuwu|"

Nariti<n>rona llao alau| lattu' rilopinna| Engkamani madduappulo lattu' rilopinna| Datué riLuwu| Nalopi baiccu'menna| natuju naola| Iana natonangngi llao riwanuwanna| Ianaro nangkasi pajung paimeng riBoné| Naé' pajung cella'sia| pajunna Datué riLuwu| rialaé| Agana ritellana| tania kupomabusung| La Te<n>risukki' Mappajungngé|

Iatona mangkau' riBoné| nasisala toMa<m>pué| toBoné| Nasiwangungang musu| Nasiosengngenna| Nakua siduppa riattanna Itterrung| Naribuanna toMa<m>pué| naripalattu' riwanuwanna| Nassu'na ArumMa<m>pu manyo<m>pa| sorongeng sebbu-kkati| "Élo'mu élo'| Aru<m>Poné| kko temmupassara-mmenna ana'ku' pattaroku'|"

Makkedani Aru<m>Poné| "Kupalimuo| ArumMampu| mutudappalili riBoné| Temmacaddiko riBoné| Temmuacinnaiang ulawettasa'| pattola mala<m>pé'| wara<m>para-mmala<m>pé'| Mupasengngangngi torimu<n>rimmu|"

Nainappana ritelli' ArumMa<m>pu| Purai ritelli' ArumMa<m>pu| e<n>rengngé lilina| lisuni Aru<m>Poné riwanuwanna|

Naduappulo pitu-taunna mangkau'| nateppai lasa| Napaddeppungenna toBoné| nakkeda "Maserro lasaku' |naé' dékkua matéa'| ianatu ana'ku| riasengngé riLa Ulio| ianatu tolawa'|"

Purai mappaseng| massialamotoni|

6

Mappajungngéna poana'| Matinroé rItterrung| Naia pawélainnana| Mappajungngé Boté'ési Mangkau'| riBoné| Apa' ia riappasengngeng| ri<n>cajiangngéngngi| tania kupomabusung| riLa Ulio[9]| aseng rialéna| Riasengngi malolomupa| namaloppo| Tallebbi pituisia pa<m>puléna| Nassisulléngi pa<m>puléna| Aga naritellana Boto'é|

Ianaé arung mapparessang| mappattuju| Iatona riaseng mélori ssawung| riaseng matanang|

Ianaé Boto'é| riaseng siala ana'na| Arungngé riPattiro|ritellaé Magadingngé| riaseng Wé Te<n>riwéwang| Da<n>raé pattellarenna|

Ana'na Magadingngé| mapowawinéi Boté'é| najajina| tania upomabusung| riasengngé La Te<n>rirawé| ritellaé Bongkangngé| Najajitona| tania upomabusung| riasengngé La Icca'| Najajitona| tania upomabusung| retella'é Te<n>ripauwang| najajitona| tania upomabusung| riasengngé| I Lémpe'|

Ianaé| Boté'éwé| arung mmula riranreng| riKajao Laliddong| Iato-

[p. 10]

-na| arung makkuluada| Karaéngngé riGowa| riasengngé Daéng Mata<n>ré| Iatona nariaseng adaé| sitettongenna| Sudeng| La Téariduni| Iatona bbétai| Datué riLuwu| mo<n>rona riCe<n>rana| nasilaong karaéngngé| riasengngé Daéng Bonto| ana'na Daéng Mata<n>ré| Nalanni Lise' Karaéngngé| malani Lappa Aru<m>Poné|

Ma'bawinétoni riMa<m>pu Boté'é| siala Wé Tenrigau'| ana'na ArumMa<m>pu| riasengngé Daéng Palimpu|

Naiatonaé Boté'é| Mangkau' riBoné| nalao mai| Karaéngngé riGoa| namula malla'éngngi| tanaé riBoné| Iana nariaseng| nasitudangeng| Karaéngngé riGoa| Aru<m>Poné| riattanna Laccokkong| Nasiwuno toGowaé| toBoné| Naé' rékkowa toBoné pawetta| Karaéngngé riGoa| passa<m>puriwi| Naé' rékkowa toGowaé| pawetta Aru<m>Poné passa<m>puriwi| Iatona Mangkau'| narisilaongang| riKaraéngngé riGoa| Nalai sebbu-katinna toWajo'é| kuwa riasengngé riTopacceddo|

9 It is not clear why the copyist writes *ri-* before the name La Ulio here and in the previous chapter.

Naia genne'na| duappulo lima-ttaunna| Mangkau' riBoné| ripasipulunni toBoné| nakkeda "Maélo'ka' mennang| paléssoriwi akkarungengngé| ana'ku'| riasengngé La Te<n>rirawé|"

Samakadoni toBoné| nalanti'ni ana'na| pitungngesso pitu<m>penni| Purai nalanti' ana'na| nonno'ni risalassa'é| Puatta Boté'é| Maddua wanuwani| Engkana llao riMa<m>pu ribainéna| engkana llao riBoné|

Iana Boté'é| magelliwi ana'uréna| riasengngé La Pau<n>ru| Nagellitoi sapposisenna| makkarungngé riPaccing| riasengngé La Mulia| Maélo' mappawakkangangngi aléna| ritoMa<m>puwé| nariéllau adda<m>pengngeng| Apa' nasitujuangngi| paléléna wenni Boté'é| riMa<m>pu| apa' teppasidapi'pi| ada toMampué nonno'ni Boté'é ssawung| Naitani sapposisenna| ana'uréna| Nawaruwanni gelli paimeng| Apa' lisuni paimeng riBoné| Nasipakkedana La Pau<n>ru| e<n>rengngé La Mulia| "Madécéngngi marolata'kua riKajaoé| mappawakkangangngi aléta'| Iamuapasa| méllau adda<m>pangangngi'|"

Apa' nadapi'ni Itterrung| nagilinna massailé| Boté'é| naitani sapposisenna| e<n>rengngé ana'uréna| nasenni aléna riola| maélo' rijallo'| Nassurona palésso'i[10] ulérenna| Aga naseddinni aléna| La Pau<n>ru| dé' alepperrenna| majjallo'menni| Sipulireng Boté'é| I La Mulia| tau lai-mmanasa ppuliriwi| Riasengngi Boté'é| Mati<n>roé rItterrung|

7

Mati<n>roéna rItterrung| poana'i| Mati<n>roé riGucinna| Bongkangngéna Mangkau'| apa' ripakkaru-mmémengngi| rituona <n>cajiangngéngngi| Tania upomabusung| La Te<n>rirawé aseng rialéna| Bongkangngé| Bongkangngé pattellarenna| Iana ma'bawiné riTimurung siala Arungngé riTimurung| riasengngé Te<n>ripakkiu| Na dua ana'na| Séuwa[11] riaseng La Maggalatung| iana maté malolo| Séuwa riaseng Punna riSo<m>pa| ia ripanguju mattola riTimurung| Maté rijallo'-

10 *palésso'i*. In the manuscript, two *aksara* after the *pa-* have been obliterated and the rest of the word written in above, apparently by another hand.

11 *séuwa*. The *-u-* in this word has been neatly added above the line of the text by another hand. Its omission is a clear scribal error.

[p. 11]

-i I[12] Da Kalula asenna jallo'éngngi|

Ianaé Bongkangngé| tenrissessia macca| Ripujisia manyame-kkininnawa| Ripuji pa'baruga| Ripujito malempu| Ripujito malabo| Ripujito pasawung| Ripujito maélo' mappasiuno| Riasettoi naéloriwi| séajing mariawana| Riasettoi mmala ada ritomatowanna| Riasengngikia maserro gelli| kko-masai'i|

Iatona mangkau'| nataro Tomakkajennangeng| Nakkajennangeng jowana| anakarunna| Joa' wanuwaé| Anyakkélaié| Sininna poasengngé panré| Sininnato pakkammo makku<n>raié| pa<m>pulé'é| Parala ajué| Pakkeddé'é| Pangolo anréngngé| Pallogé'é|Iatonana mula engka ballili'|

Ianaé Bongkangngé| Mangkau'| nangka Karaéngngé riGowa| muttama' riBoné| ssawung nariéwa mattaro| riKaraéngngé| siratu katinna| Na toPanyula'é séwanuwa| natangkerrangngi| Cella' manu'na Karaéngngé| Bakka'-mattemu manu'na Aru<m>Poné| Nariuno manu'na Karaéngngé| siratu kati rilalettoro'|

Naiatona Mangkau'| namallébu toriAjangale'é| makkatenni riBoné| Nabétai Awo| Téko| nabéta manettoni riAttassalo| Baliéng paimeng|

Iatonaé makkarung nangka Tellumpoccoé| la<n>rengngi babanna riGoa| makkatenni riBoné| naripatudappalili'na Karaéngngé| mmutamai nakkuana riattanna Méru| siduppa Mangkasa'é| toBoné| Nattebbanna pitu-ngngesso| Nainappana tauwé| makkeda-<a>da nasiajenna toBoné| toGoaé| Nannessana llao toBoné| wiring riattanna saloé| Tangka nalalo manai'|

Iatona Bongkangngé| Mangkau' nangka Addatuwang riSompa| riSawitto| naripassu' nalao mai riBoné|

Iatona Mangkau'| nakkappuéng toSoppéngngé rilale<m>panuwa| Nasaurenna ArusSoppé<n>riaja| ritella'é Mabbéluwa'é| Nalaona mai riBoné| Naiana Mabbéluwa'é kkonisa riBoné ma'bawiné| siala ana'daranna Arungngé riBoné| riasengngé Te<n>ripauwang| Najaji<a>nni riasengngé I Dakke'| ritella'é Lébaé| Iatona riaseng Datué riMario| Nallakkaina

12 Matthes appears to have added a *pallawa* and crossed through the first *aksara* of this name, thus bringing the text into line with other versions. In his notes, he suggests the form Dakalulla is a contraction of Daéng Kalulla.

ana'daranna Aru<m>Poné| tania kupomabusung| riasengngé Wé Lé<m>pe'| siala Maddanrengngé| riasengngé La Saliwu| sappowékkaruamui| Iana ncajiangngi| taniya kupomabusung| riasengngé La Tenriruwa| Matinroé riBantaéng| aseng rimaténa|

Iatona Matinroé riGucié| mangkau' nangka mai mmuttama riBoné| ana'uréna Karaéngngé riGowa| Daéng Pabéta asenna| Ana'uréna Karaéngngé| engkaé mai riBoné| puramani duppai tomajjallo'| Naritellana ritoBoné| Daéng Patobo'| Maddi-Bonéni| Daéng Patobo'| Nangkana Karaéngngé| riasengngé Daéng Bonto| ttériwi Boné| Na kuwana riCellu ssoré| Nammusu'na toBoné| Mangkasa'é| Namalo'na Daéng Bontoipo| Na lima-ngngesso tauwé matebbang| Nalisu Karaéngngé riwanuwanna|

Naduwa-ttaung purana mammusu' riCellu| nangkasiro mai| Karaéngngé riGowa| ttériwi Boné| Nakuwa riWalenna ttaro bénténg| Nattebbanna toBo-

[p. 12]

-né| toGowaé| Malo' bessiwi Daéng Patobo'| Nalebbi pitungngesso mattebbang| Nateppani lasa[13] Karaéngngé| Nariparéwe' riwanuanna| namaténa tengkenne' duwa<m>puleng|

Nangkasiro mai Karaéngngé Daéng Parukka| ttériwi Boné| Nabbalina toriAjangale'é| ia maneng| Naia toTimurungngé| napabétai ana'na| pattarona| nalao mai alau riBoné| ma'deddessangngi aléna| Na makkunraimani garé' riaseng| mmonro riTimurung| silaongngana'na| Naia Lima<m>panuaé| Rilaué| kkoi riCinennung| nawawa pattarona| nauttama ma'dedderrangngi aléna| woroané riBoné|

Appa'balittoni toriAwamPoné| Nakona riPappolo| Karaéngngé ttaro bénténg| Tépui bénténna| nasosongini Boné| Natelloni Bukaka sépué'| enrengngé riTakké Ujung| Apa' lésanni essoé| maélo'ni ma'dimpa Mangkasa'é| Riarupani ritoBoné| Ribuanni Mangkasa'é| Nadapi'ni llari Garaéngngé[14]| Kkui riCempaé| naripeppe'na Mangkasa'é| Riwettani Karaéngngé| La Turu asenna <m>pettaéngngi|Karaéngngémani riasengngé Daéng Padulung| nattingara toGowaé| Massuroni Karaéngngé

13 *lasa*. The second *aksara* seems to have been originally *–si*, but this has been crossed out and *–sa* added above in another hand.
14 *Garaéngngé*. A mistake for Karaéngngé. Another hand has written a faint *Ka–* above the first *aksara*.

riTallo'| llao riBoné| Naia napoada surona| Karaéngngé riTallo'| "Duwa puammeng| séuwa muwetta ritappéré'| séuwa muwetta ritengngana padangngé| Naé maélo'nakkeng ridécéngngé| Téanakkeng rija'é|"

Makkedani Kajaolaliddong| "Laona makkoniritu adammu| bajapa matu' kuassu' riKaraéngngé|"

Pappa' bajaé| massu'ni Kajaolaliddong| Kkuni macceppa' Karaéngngé| Napurana sikado-ngngadanna| Purai macceppa'| Karaéngngé riTallo'| toBoné| riasengngé Daéng Padulung| Daéng Patobo'si ripakkarung nriGowa|

Iatona Bongkangngéwé| makkarung riBoné| nasisala Datué riLuwu| riasengngé Sangkaria| Apa' téai paimeng Luwué| <m>panuai Cé<n>rana| Natérisi paimeng Cé<n>rana| Luwué| Agana wékka duwana tanaé riCé<n>rana| riala-bessi ritoBoné| Ianaé| namula ata toUnyi'é riBoné|

Iatonaé Bongkangngé| mangkau' riBoné| nasellao Arung Matowaé riWajo'| riasengngé toUddamang| Nasellaoto Arungngé riSoppéng| ritellaé Pollipué| Appasibuni riCé<n>rana| kkuni sita masséajing| Iana nassiturusi| passéajingngéngngi <tanana>| Nakkeda madécéngngi' sita riTimurung| Nakupa tépu pautta'| ritépunna ulengngé|"

Apa' nadapini esso natanraé siduppani riTimurung| Engka manenni toBoné sílili'| engka manettoni toWajo'é sílili'| engka manettoni toSoppéngngé sílili'| Kkuni riBoné ttaro baruga| nakkuna ttaro sawung| Apa' o<m>po' loloni ulengngé| sipulunni toBoné| toWajoé| toSoppéngngé| Situdangenni Aru<m>Poné| Arung Matowaé riWajo'| Datué riSoppéng| napassiajingngi tanana| iatellu| Kuwaétosia| padaorané sina –ssiama<ng>é| Bonéna macoa| ana' tengngai Wajo| paccucungngi Soppéng| Naina-

[p. 13]

-ppa sitelli'| Naia nassitelliri| " Tebbaiccukengngé| Tessiacinnangngé ulawettasa'| Pattola malampé'| Waramparang malappa'|" Nainappana mallamumpatu| Nasenni tanana Tellumpoccoé|

Ianaé arung maserro riélori| ritoBoné| Maserroto riuddani| Naduwa-ttaung purana mallamumpatu| Tellumpoccoé| nateppani lasa Bongkangngé| Napasipulunni toBoné| "Ia mennang kupoadadakko| anrikku'naritu ttolawa'|"

Natampaini anrinna| tania kupomabusung| riasengngé La Icca'| Nakkedana| "Ia kupoadakko-nri'| madodonna'é| Atutuiwi gau'mu| apa' iko ritu kuélorang mangkau'| rékko matéa'| Iatopa kupoadakko| rékko matéa'| naleppe'na winru'-tomatéu'| uwélorangngi mupowawiné ipa'mu| Iomisio maupe'| nangka ana'mu riArutTimurung| Kuélorangngi namupoawiseng| Masulitu makkunrai kkuaé tujunna| enrengngé nawa-nawanna| Nabara' mumuruppengngi tanaé riBoné|"

Purai mappaseng| masialangngi| Riasenni Matinroé riGucié|

8

Matinroéna riGucié| popadaorowanéi| Matinroé riAddénénna| Ia pawélainana Matinroé riGucié| tania kupomabusung| La Icca'na makkarung riBoné| apa' ia ripasengngang rikakana| Naia purana nawinru' tomaténa| Matinroé riGucinna| rilanti'ni|

Purai rilanti'| napowinéni Arungngé riTimurung| Tenripakkiu| Najajina riasengngé| tania upomabusung| La Tenripale' To Akke<m>péang pattellarenna| Najajitona| tania kupomabusung| Wé Tenrijello'| Iana ritella Makkalaru'é| Engkatopa séuwa| malolomupa namaté|

Iana Mangkau' riBoné| tania upomabusung| riasengngé La Icca'| nangkaro mai Karaéngngé riGowa| ttériwi Boné| Naé' tellattu'toni nalisu| Karaéngngé|

Ianaé arung| tania kupomabusung| tenrisseng rinawa-nawa| Iamua naripauttama risure'é| annessanamua gau'é|

Ianaé Mangkau'| nammulana toBoné| tessiseng siéwa ada| Nagillinna[15] ArupPallenna| riasengngé La Panaongi| To Pawawoi pattellarenna| Naripalina kuwa riSidénréng| Apa' mangingngini ttudang riSidénréng| maélo'muani llisu riBoné| méllau addampeng| Risurosi maddé' llao manai' riBuki'é| Riolani nariuno| ArupPallenna Riunotoi|Arungngé riPaccing Riunotoi| Arungngé riAwamPoné riasengngé To Saliwu| Riawang Riunotoni| Maddanrengngé riPalakka| riasengngé To Saliwu Riwawo| Maégato arung toBoné| riuno| Nasalossoni tau tessalossorennaépa| Napaté'ni tau teppatérennaépa| Onconni tessisenna siéwa ada toBoné| naé' dé'pa gau'|

15 *Nagillinna.* A mistake for Nagellinna.

Iamua garé' nawinru wette'reng| Engka séuwa esso| nangka toBoné| nalaong naré'-aré'i awisenna| Naridapi'na namaélo'na tauwé

[p. 14]

- <m>punoi| Nalarina tauwé| Iamani wawinéna tauwé nauno| Nainappana massellang| Napanréiwi api sipué' Boné| gangkanna Matajang| lattu' urai'| riMacégé| Natasséa-séana| toBoné| Iamani| arung <e>ngkapa| <m>pokke'ngaléna| nalao maniang riMajang| Makkedani Puatta'| riMajang| "Maragotu mai|"

Makkedai toBoné| "Tekkisseng palappa-lappai Puang| Tellommunosa[16] muitai monorang| wanuwaé riBoné|"

Apa' tellonni Puatta riMajang| nata<m>puini arona nakkeda| "Malebborang énnajai lumuna Puakku'|" Naé' dé'pa adammeng| napoada toBoné| "Assurosao mmalangnga' riMa<m>pu| anauréku| riasengngé Da Malaka| Apa' iamenniritu| Arung Matoa|"

Makkedai tauwé| "Engkamui monorang riPalakka Puang|"

Rilaona rialai| Temmai<tta>to nangkaro mai| Makkedai Da Malaka| "Aga Puang tassuro mmalangnga'|"

Makkedai Puatta' riMajang| "Iatu llaomu romai| Temmuitaga| rumpu apié riBoné|"

Makkedaa[17]| Da Malaka| "Nasia Puwang| uwitamua|"

"Ianatu| uwassuro mmalako| pékkoni| nawa-nawammu|"

Mekkomoi| Da Malaka| Nawékka-tellumana| riéwa ada| riPuatta' riMajang| nainappana makkeda| "Matau'ka' Puang| Madécé-mmua| rékko passesse'mua| limpoa'|"

Makkedai| Puatta' riMajang| "Idi' sikuwaéwé| Tagerro séuwamuni| tauru|"

Makkedani Da Malaka| "Makkoniritu adatta' Puwang| Naé' dé' salai| nadapi' nawa-nawaku'| Iamani| tapassu'é nalengngi'ang lebbi'|na tanaé| Namau puatta' riolo| nalebbiranga-mmémessa tanaé| nawatakkaléna| maui tennapoade'| mappassué| Ia'nasia| mulai gau'| kupassui anauréu'|"

---

16 *Tellommunosa.* The second *aksara* has been added above the line, apparently by the original scribe.

17 *Makkedaa.* A mistake for *Makkedai.*

Jaji Da Malakana| patetto-ngngada| Nasuroiwi ana'uréna| makkedaé| "Assuko| tanikoritu sengngangke' tanaé|"

Nalattu'na torisuroé| Kkumoi ritanaé| napoléi| napalattu'ni risuroangngéngngi| Tennapoada manettopa| nariunona|Suroé| Nainappana| tello manengngi bolaé| riBoné| riLalebbata|

Aga paissenni| Puatta' riMajang| dé'na bola riLalebbata| Makkedani Puatta'| riMajang| "Uléka'| kalaki'| muwawa riBoné| naia' llao| sipulireng eppou' Makkullénaritu| uwéwa siuno| Laona| taniana arung|"

Makkedai Da Malaka| "Laotoa' matu'| apa' pura manenni| mattaro ada| tagerro séuwa taurui"|

Lao manenni tauwé| riBoné| Ripoléiniria| iamani rialé-aléna| Inappai naita tau tebbe'é| nalluruini| maéga tau tauno[18]| Makkomaniro garé'| gau'na Iasi nalurui| iasi llari| Ia nabokori| iasi mmolaiwi| narang puru'na

[p. 15]

Llaomuni riaddénénna| ssanré| Nalaona Puatta' riMajang| sila'i| ulunna| eppona| namaténa| Nariasenna Matinroé riAddénénna| Makkedatoi taué| To<m>pawaéngngi| Salassana| Seppulo séuwa| taunna mangkau'| iamatona| namaté|

9

Matinroé riAddénénna| sapposisengngi Matinroé| riBettung| Ia maténana| Matinroé riAddénénna| sipulunni| toBoné| riPuatta' riMajang| nasipattangngareng| naningngaré'na| tapatetto-ngarung|

Napatettonna élo'| Arungngé riMajang| Makkedai| Arungngé riMajang| "Nalaleng iagasa tala arung| tenna eppoo[19] La Pattawe'| ana'na ArupPallenna| eppona Makkale<m>pié|"

Najajina samaturu' Arung toBoné| kkado| ArukKajuna| ripatettong| Arung| riBoné| nariasenna| ArumPoné| Iana riaseng| La Pattawe'| Nabbawinéna| ArumPoné| siala Arungngé riMampu| Nana'na| taniya upomabusung riasengngé Tenritappu|

---

18 *tauno*. A mistake for *nauno*.

19 *eppoo*. A mistake for *eppou'*.

Nabbawinéna| tania upomabusung| La Tenriruwa| siala massapposiseng| riasengngé Dakke'| Najajiangngi| tania upomabusung| riasengngé La Tenrisui| Naé' dé' ridapi'| riéngkalinga| paunna rilale-ngakkarungenna| Iamua makkedaé| pitu-ttaummui| mangkau' riBoné| Nalao riBuluku<m>pa| nako nateppa lasa| naiamatona| mpawai nasiasenna

10

Matinroé riBettung| Poana'i| Matinroé riSidénréng| Apa' iana| ana'na Matinroé riBettung| riasengngé I Tenriu<m>pu| iana riaseng| Aru<m>Poné|

Ianaé mangkau'| napatettong ArupPitu| Naia Matowaé| riTobojong[20]| riasenni ArutTibojong| Matowaé riTa'| riasenni ArutTa'| Matowaé riUjung| riasenni ArungNGujung| Matowaé riPoncéng| riasenni ArupPoncéng| Matowaé riTanété| riasenni ArutTanété| Matowaé riMacégé| riasenni ArumMacégé|

Makkedai| Aru<m>Poné| "Ia mennang| kupatettommu| ArupPitué| maélo'mua'| muampiri| rilao<n>rumaé| enrengngé ritoanana| arungngé riBoné| apa' makkunraia| Enrengngé maélo'ka'| musapparang lise'na salassaé| tatteré-teré| Naékia| upatettommu ArupPitu| temmulawiriwi| tanaé riBoné| temmuaddi<m>pa sunrang| temmamanako riana'mu| rékko tekkuissengngi| sangadinna rékko situdangengngi'| idi'maneng| wijanna Mappajungngé| nasituru' makkarungngé riBoné| Nappasisa llao| inappatonisa| llalo pa-

[p. 16]

-mmanamu| riana'mu| rieppomu|"

Iatonaé| makkarung riBoné| nangka Karaéngngé| riGowa| ttérang asellengeng| Ajatappareng| napaolai| osong| Nalao Tellu<m>poccoé| duppaiwi| Mangkasa'é| laona ssu'| Karaéngngé| riwanuwanna|

Nasitaummua| nangkasi Karaéngngé| ttériwi Pandang-Pandang| Nalaosi| Tellu<m>poccoé| Nasiduppa rilau'na| Bulu' Sitoppo'| nasiabbaléccorang| tauwé| Naribuanna| Tellu<m>poccoé| Napada-llaona| riwanuwanna| narussa'na| atTellu<m>poccongengngé| Boné| Wajo| Soppéng|

20 *Tobojong*. A mistake for *Tibojong*.

Nasétaung| marussa' Tellu<m>poccoé| nangkasi Karaéngngé| ttériwi Soppéng| Tennalaona| toBoné| toWajo'é| bbaliwi toSoppéngngé| Naribétana| Soppéng| nasellenna toSoppéngngé|

Nasétaung| sada'na| toSoppéngngé| nangkasi Karaéngngé| ttériwi Wajo| Nanga<n>rona toWajo'é| naripauttamasi sada'|

Nasétaung purana| sada'| toWajo'é| nalao Aru<m>Poné| riSidé<n>réng| maélo' makkutanangngi| akkuwa-uwanna asellengengngé| Nalattu'mua riSidé<n>réng| nasellenna| Nakotona riSidé<n>réng| nateppai lasa| Na iana <m>pawai| Nasera[21] taunna| Mangkau' riBoné| namaté| Nariasenna| Matinroé riSidénréng|

11

Mati<n>roé riSidénréng| sapposisengngi| Mati<n>roé riBantaéng| Ia pawélaina| Mati<n>roé riSidénreng| sipulunni toBoné| Naia nassiturusi| ArupPalakka narutto riPattiro| apa' eppona wali-wali| Mappajungngé| Mappajungngé| ArupPalakkana| ripasekkoreng| pajung| Tania upomabusung| La Tenrirua| aseng rialéna| Iatona| ripésonaiang| alé| ritoBoné| paoppang|paléngengngi| tanaé riBoné|

Apa' tekkenne'topa| tellu<m>puleng makkarung| nangkana Karaéngngé| ttériwi Boné| riMusu' Sellengngé| Ma'bénténni| riCellu| Mangkasa'é| ma'béntéttoni| riPallетté| karaéngngé| Rita<n>réréanganni asellengeng| toBoné|

Makkedai Aru<m>Poné| "Laona ia mennang| mupésonaia'| paoppang|paléngengngi tanaé riBoné| mupasekkori pajung| Naé nata<n>réréangangngi'| décéng| Karaéngngé| Madécéngngiasa| taceppa'| asellengengngé| Apa' ia| uluadatta'| riolo| riKaraéngngé| ia llolongang| décéng| tajang| ia mappaita| Nakkedana Karaéngngéwé|'Uwasengngi décéng| tajang| makkatennikku'| riagamana| Na'bié'| Nakkedatopa Karaéngngé| Rékko mutarimai| adakku'

21 *Nasera*. Matthes has corrected this to *Naséra*.

[p. 17]

dua maraja| Gowamua| naBoné| tapadana makkasiwiang| riDéwata Séuwaé'|" Makkedatopi| Aru<m>Poné| "Rékkoromi| tettaririmai[22]| a<da>ada[23] madécénna| Karaéngngé| tatongengiwi| natelloppi' matu| nanyo<m>pa| atani'| asenna| Narékko tatarimai| ada madécénna| Karaéngngé| nawélaiyyangngi' ada| matti parimeng| muasengnga'| téa méwai| siwuno| Inappatonisia| kuéwa| rékko nawélaiangnga'| ada|"

Samatéani| toBoné| kkadoiwi| asellengengngé|

Mekko'muni| Aru<m>Poné| apa' nase'dinni| Aru<m>Poné| lainna| kédona toBoné| Nalaimuni| aléna Aru<m>Poné| nalao riPattiro| Tau rialénamani| mmolaiwi| Apa' llattu'i| riPattiro| naéwasi ada| toPattiroé| téamessi mmolaiwi| asellengengngé| Mekko'muni Puatta'| naté' risalassa'é| ma'dedde'| Rangeng rialéna|tomanisa| nasilaongang| Ana'na| pattarona| napaté' maneng| risalassa'é|

Naia lésso'na| llao riPattiro| Aru<m>Poné| sipulunni toBoné| Ia nassiturusi| passu'éngngi| Aru<m>Poné| Nassurona toBoné| llao riPattiro| na To Alaung| asenna| risuroé| Nalattu'na| To Alaung| riPattiro| té'ni manai'| risalassa'é| Makkedai| "To Alaung ngAmang| Ia nasuroangnga'| toBoné Amang| Tanidi'naritu| téaio| idi'naritu| téaikkeng| Natujuni bali| <a>tammu| riBoné| muwélaiwi|"

Makkedai Puatta'| "O To Alaung| massakkakoitu| téawi toBoné| uwélorinna muaritu| toBoné| Kuripaitai décéng| e<n>rengngé tajang| kumaélo'-tongenna| ré<n>ré'ko| ritajangngé| mutéa mennang| Naé akkatenninno| mi| rinawa-nawa pettammu| Ulaotonasa| ritajanna paranyalaé| Déwata Séuwaé| riNa'bié"|

Purai makkeda| To Alaungeng| <n>réwe'ni riBoné| Iasi nassiturusi| toBoné| ArutTimurungngéna| napakkarung riBoné| Apa' ana'nai| Mati<n>roé riAddénénna| tania upomabusung| riasengngé| La Tenripale'| aseng rialéna| To Akke<m>péang| aseng <n>riana'na| Pawélaimenni| nariasenna| Mati<n>roé riTello'| Iana makkarung| naparéwai| toBoné| rimusu sellengngé|

Naia| lésso'na nalao| To Alaungang| llao riBoné| massuro ma-

22 *Tettaririmai.* The copyist seems to have begun the *aksara* for the second *-ri-* as a *-ma-*, but then corrected it to add emphasis.

23 *a<da>ada.* The repetition of the word seems to be intended.

[p. 18]

-tonisa| Puatta'| llao riKaraéngngé| koriPalletté| Lattu'i riPalletté surona| massurotonisa| Karaéngngé| llao riPattiro| Karaéng Pettung| risuro| Aga lettu'nana| Aga lettu'nana[24]| Karaéng Pettung| riPattiro| ripasiléwoni| Puatta'| ritoPattiroé| e<n>rengngé ritoBulu'é| Naruppaini| najjallo'| Nabuanni| Sébulu'é| e<n>rengngé toPattiroé| Napakkappoi| riBulu'é| riMaroanging|

Puraikuwa| malliwenni| riPalletté| Puatta'| sita Karaéngngé| Karaéngngémenni| Pettung| mon<n>roangngi Pattiro| Aga lettu'ni| Puatta'| riKaraéngngé| makkedani Karaéngngé| "Madécénnibéla| laona| llaoko mai| Naiasa| ukkutana riko| kéga| gangkanna| anurialému| Mauékko temmakkarung| riBoné| mupoanumua| Apa' uwaseng| mupoanu Boné| naé léléni|"

Makkedai Puatta'| "Anu rialéu'na| kuwaé Palakka| e<n>rengngé Pattiro| e<n>rengngé Awa<m>Poné| Naia| Mario-Riwawo| anu rialénatosa| awisekku'|"

Makkedai Karaéngngé| "Sada'no| naiatonasotu| sékkuwaé| mutama' sada'| mupoanué| Boné teppoatao| Goa teppoatao|"

Makkedai Puatta'| "Sada'é mémenna'| Karaéng| kulao mai|"

Nainappasi makkeda| Karaéngngé| "Uwissemmua| mupoanu Palletté| Naé' tettongennai| batéu'| uwasenni anukku'| naé <a>nukku'nisia| Palletté| kuwérékko"|

Nainappasi| riwéréng Puatta'| riKaraéngngé| appala baludu'| rikoi' ulawettasa'| sikati berre'na|

Makkedai Puatta'| "Rékko ia Karaéng| muwéréngnga'| tekkusilaonganna| toBoné| mméwao| téawa' mmalai|"

Makkedai Karaéngngé| "Muisse<n>ritu baiseng| ade'nai torioloé| rékko sitai passéajingenna| engkatosia| nawi<n>ru' assitang| sullé alosi séire'| éwulu sila<m>pa|"

Makkedai Puatta'| "Uwanuritu| Karaéng| lanako adammu"|

24 *aga lettu'nana*. The repetition of these words is a mistake.

Puraikuwa| inappani| makkuluada| Puatta'| Karaéngngé| Puatta' Mati<n>roé| riBantaéng Karaéngngé riGoa| Mula Sellengngé| Karaéngngé riTello'| Mula Sellengngé|

Ianaé| akkuluadangenna| Makkedai Karaéngngé| "Iana tappasabbiang

[p. 19]

riDéwata Séuwaé| taniapa wijammeng| makkarung riGowa| riTallo'| temmupoanui anummu| murigau' bawang| ripadammu tau| Naé' rékkua engka ja'| ttujuo| ti<m>pa'i tange'mu| kutama rija'mu|"

Makkedatonisia| Mati<n>roé riBantaéng| "O Karaéng| temmarunu' wesséu'| tessekka bilakku'| tenriti<m>pa' balawo| rita<m>pukku'| naé dékkuwa| engka tujui| tanaé riGowa| Mau sébatammua awo| uwappangi kulao| matturi ssu'| riperri'mu Karaéng| Lettu' ritorimunrimmu| ritorimunrikku|tosa| rékkowa tenriwélaia-mmuakkeng ada| rikkeng tobaiccu'é|"

Kkunié akkuluadanna| Matinroé riBantaéng| na Karaéngngé| Purai macceppa' Puatta'| na Karaéngngé| lisuni paimeng riPattiro| Na lima<m>penni| purana macceppa'| Karaéngngé| na Puatta' Matinroé riBantaéng| natello Boné| narimusu' sellengngé| Manyo<m>pani toBoné| naripasada'na|Nalisuna Karaéngngé| riwanuanna|

Nalésso'mua llao Karaéngngé| narisurona meddé'| Matinroé riBantaéng| ritoBoné| Nalaona ssu' riMangkasa| Naana' riDato' Bandang| Nai aseng Jawana| Matinroé riBantaéng| riDato' Bandang| Adama aseng Jawana| Matinroé riBa<nta>éng|

Maittai mmonro riDato' Bandang| Ripangiléni onrong| riKaraéngngé| Naia naélori| naonroi| riBantaéng| Agana kkuna riwawa| Na kuna mmonro| Matinroé riBantaéng| nakkuna narapi' umuru'na| nariasenna Matinroé riBantaéng|

12

Matinroé riBantaéng| ripassu'| sapposisengngi Matinroé riTello'| Iana ripassu'na Matinroé riBantaéng| ArutTimurunna| nassiturusi toBoné| napakkarung| Apa' ana'na Matinroé riAddénénna| riArungngé riTimurung| Ianaé Aru<m>Poné| tania upomabusung| riaseng La <Ten>ripale'| To Akke<m>péang pattellarenna|

Ianaé mangkau'| naparéwe'i toBoné| riMusu' Sellengngé| Naritellona Boné| nanganrona toBoné| tenriala| sebbukatinna| tenriéllau rebbabaténa| tenrirappatoi| Manyo<m>pana toBoné| ripasada'muni napura| Naiakia tudappalili'manenni|

Naia puranana ripasada' toBoné| ripasada' sépalili'| laotonisa Karaéngngé| riwanuanna| ArutTimurunna| mangkau' riBoné| Pawélaimani| nariasenna Matinroé riTallo'|

Naé| duwai sijajing| Matinroé riTallo'| Anrinna riaseng| tania upomabusung| Wé Tenrijello'| Iana ritella Makkalaru'é| Iana Makkalaru'é| sia-

[p. 20]

-la Arungngé riSumali| riasengngé La Pancai| Najajina riasengngé| La Maddaremmeng| Salih aseng Jawana| Iana ripakkarung riTimurung| Nariala Pattiro| iatona Mappakkalaru'é[25] Arung riPattiro| Séuwatopa anrinna| tania kupomabusung| La Maddaremmeng| riaseng Te<n>ria<m>pareng| Iana makkarung riCellu| Séuwatopa anrinna| riaseng La Tenriaji| To Senrima aseng riana'na| Iana ripakkarung riAwamPoné| Iatona riaseng| Pawélaié riSiang|

Nallakkaina| tania upomabusung| riasengngé Wé Tenrisui| siala La Pottobune'| arungngé riTana-Tengnga| Najajianni riasengngé| Da Unru| tania kupomabusung| riasengngé La Tenritatta| To Unru' aseng riana'na| tammana'| Enrengngé| Da Tenrigerra| puttatoi| e<n>rengngé Da O<m>po' tammana'| E<n>rengngé Da Émba| Enrengngé riasengngé| tania kupomabusung| riasengngé[26]| Wé Pappolobonga[27]| Da U<m>pi aseng riana'na| Iana riaseng| Madda<n>rengngé|

---

25 *Mappakkalaru'é*. This should be *Makkalaru'é* as twice previously in this paragraph.

26 *riasengngé*. This repetition is unnecessary.

27 *Pappolobonga*. She is usually known as *Mappolobombang*.

Nasétaung purana ssada'| toBoné| nalao ssu'| riMangkasa| Nasita| Dato' riBandang| riasengngé| Abeddulla| aseng Jawana| Aru<m>Poné| Iana Arung manyame-kkininnawa| Riasettoi pabbaruga| riasettoi maserro pallao<n>ruma|

Iana siala| ana'na Matinroé riSide<n>réng| ritellaé| Kaunangngé| Ana'na ritellaé Dabe'| Dabe'na situmaé| ana'na Karaéngngé riGowa| Mula Sellengngé| Daéng Mattola asenna| ana'na Karaéngngé| potumaiéngngi| Dabe'| Naé' tennawette'pa dara| namaté| Jaji dé'na ana'padana| Aru<m>Poné|

Ianaé| arung mallao-lisu riKaraéngngé| maittawégangngi| rékko telluttaungngi| nalaosi ssu'|

Apa' nasitujuangngi| llaona ssu'| riMangkasa| lattu'i ssu'| riMangkasa'| kuani nateppa lasa| iana lasa <m>pawai| Agana kuana riTallo'| rilemme'| nariasenna Matinroé riTallo'| Dua-ppuloi taunna| mangkau'| napawélai|

13

Matinroé riTallo'| napoanauré riwakkangngi| Matinroé riBukaka| Ia pawélainna| Matinroé riTallo'| ana'uré riwakkannana ttolai| mangkau' riBoné| Apa' ia nappasengngang| tania upomabusung| La Maddaremmeng| aseng rialéna| Salih aseng jawana| Pawélaimani| nariasenna| Mati<n>roé riBukaka|

Iana Mangkau'| nawinru' Paju<m>puté|

Iana ma'bawiné riWajo| siala| Hatija| Da Se<n>rima| aseng riana'na| ana'na Arung Matoaé| riWajo'| ritellaé| To Ala'é| Céuwamua| ana'na| Aru<m>Poné| iamua ria-

[p. 21]

-sengngé Pakkoko'é| To Akkonéng pattellarenna|

Iatonaé makkarung| napalowangngi bataé riBoné| napangésa'-alaui| napangésa'-maniangngi|

Iatona riaseng| masse' magama| Iatona massola| iagelli temmassolaé| Nasuroni massolo ncajiangngéngngi| naia napoada| Mappakkalaru'é[28]| naia napoada| "Temmakkullésa'| temmassuro-suro"

Nagillinni ncajiangngéngngi| natérini Pattiro| narappa-rappai| Llarini ssu'| Mappakkalaru'é| riKaraéngngi| Massuroni Karaéngngé riGowa| pakainge'i

Aru<m>Poné| Ritérisi riKaraéngngé| naribétasi Boné| Nabéta manai'| riCe<m>pu| Aru<m>Poné| Nariolang| naripallaleng| riwawa ssu' riMangkasaé| Nakkuna riSiang| ritaro|

Seppulo-lima-ttaunna| makkarunna| nabéta toBoné| Pawélaimani| nariaseng Matinroé riBukaka|

*

Naia ribétana| Boné riMatinroé riBukaka| pada-oroanénasi| Matinroé riBukaka| riasengngé To Se<n>rima| mmonro riBoné| Naritérisi paimeng| riKaraéngngé | Naribétasi Boné| narilaling| Iana riaseng| Béta Pasé<m>pe'| apa' kkoi te' riPasé<m>pe'| maréwang toBoné| Nariwawatona ssu'| To Senrima| nakkuanaria maté| Nariasenna Pawélaié riSiang|

Matinroémani riBukaka| mmonro riSiang| silaong toBoné rilalingngé| Ma'gangkasanié ripau| Mati<n>roé riBukaka| rionronnapasi naripau| apa' dé'na arung riBoné|

*

Ga<ng>kannamani| najennammani napatettong| Karaéngngé| mmonro riBoné| To Bala| asenna jennangiéngngi Boné| Mannessani llao atana| tauwé riBoné| riMangkasa'é|

Naseppulo-pitu-taunna| Jennang To Bala| naparéwai toBoné| Naribétasi toBoné| riMangkasa'é| Nariwettana To Bala| Iana poasengngi| Béta To Bala|

28 *Mappakkalaru'é*, here and in the next paragraph. As previously, this should be *Makkalaru'é*.

Nalliwenna riButung| Matinroé riBontoala'| Naé' ma'gangkasaniro ripau| akkatangenna tanaé riBoné| riMangkasa'é|

Ia maténa To Bala| ArungNGamalisi Jennang riBoné| Napituttaung ArungNGamali| nawawai To Boné| llao riButung| Na kuna riButung| toBoné| nangkatonaro mai| Matinroé riBontoala'| silaong Balandaé| Narialana toBoné| riMatinroé riBontoala'| ripasiala Karaéng Bontomarennu| enrengngé Mangkasa'é| iamaneng|gangkanna engkaé riButung| Tammat

Bibliography

Abdurrazak Daeng Patunru and Others 1995, *Sejarah Bone* [*History of Bone*], Yayasan Kebudayaan Sulawesi Selatan, [Ujung Pandang/Makassar].

Abidin, A.Z. 1971, 'Notes on the Lontara' as historical sources', *Indonesia* 12: 159–72. doi.org/10.2307/3350664.

Abidin, A.Z. 1985, *Wajo' pada abad XV–XVI: Suatu penggalian sejarah terpendam Sulawesi Selatan dari lontara'* [*Wajo in the XV–XVI Century: An exploration of the hidden history of South Sulawesi from Lontara'*], Penerbit Alumni, Bandung.

Andaya, L.Y. 1981, *The Heritage of Arung Palakka: A history of South Sulawesi (Celebes) in the seventeenth century*, Verhandelingen van het Koninklijk Instituut voor Taal-, Land- en Volkenkunde 91, Nijhoff, The Hague.

Auerbach, E. 1953, *Mimesis: The representation of reality in Western literature*, (trans. Willard R. Trask), Princeton University Press, Princeton, NJ.

Bakkers, J.A. 1866, 'Het leen vorstendom Boni [The dependent kingdom of Bone]', *Tijschrift voor Indische Taal-, Land- en Volkenkunde* 15: 1–204, and appendices.

Basham, A.L. 1971, *The Wonder That Was India*, 3rd edn, Fontana and Rupa & Co., Calcutta.

Behrend, T.E. (ed.) 1998, *Katalog induk naskah-naskah Nusantara, jilid 4, Perpustakaan Nasional Republik Indonesia* [*Master Catalogue of Indonesian Manuscripts, Volume 4, National Library of the Republic of Indonesia*], Yayasan Obor Indonesia and École française d'extrême orient, Jakarta.

Blok, R. 1817, *History of the Island of Celebes*, 4 vols, Calcutta Gazetter Press, Calcutta.

Budiarti, H. 2007, 'Taking and returning objects in a colonial context: Tracing the collections acquired during the Bone–Gowa military expeditions', in Pieter ter Keurs (ed.), *Colonial Collections Revisited*, Medelelingen van het Rijksmuseum voor Volkenkunde Leiden No. 36, CNMS Publications, Leiden, pp. 125–44.

Caldwell, I. 1988, South Sulawesi AD 1300–1600: Ten Bugis texts, PhD thesis, The Australian National University, Canberra.

Caldwell, I.A. 1998, 'The chronology of the king list of Luwu' to AD 1611', in K. Robinson and Mukhlis Paeni (eds), *Living through Histories: Culture, history and social life in South Sulawesi*, Department of Anthropology, Research School of Pacific and Asian Studies, The Australian National University and The National Archives of Indonesia, Canberra, pp. 29–42 [Translated as *Tapak-Tapak Waktu: Sejarah, kebudayaan, dan kehidupan sosial di Sulawesi Selatan*, Ininnawa, Makassar, 2005].

Caldwell, I. and Wellen, K. 2016, 'Family matters: Bugis genealogies and their contribution to Austronesian studies', *International Journal of Asia Pacific Studies* 12(Supp. 1): 119–41. doi.org/10.21315/ijaps2016.12.s1.6.

Cense, A.A. n.d., Beknopte beschrijving van de Boeginees en Makassaarse handscriften van de Lembaga Kebudajaan Indonesia 'Kon. Bataviaasch Genootschap van Kunsten en Wetenschappen' [Brief description of the Bugis and Makasar manuscripts of the Indonesian Cultural Foundation 'Royal Batavia Society of Arts and Sciences'], Typescript, 16 pp.

Cense, A.A. 1951, 'Enige aantekeningen over Makassaars-Boeginese geschiedschrijving [Some notes about Makasar–Bugis historiography]', *Bijdragen tot de Taal-, Land- en Volkenkunde* 107: 42–60. doi.org/10.1163/22134379-90002467.

Cense, A.A. 1966, 'Old Buginese and Macassarese diaries', *Bijdragen tot de Taal-, Land- en Volkenkunde* 122: 416–28. doi.org/10.1163/22134379-90002920.

Chairan, T., Arief Mattalitti, M. and Usmar, A. 1981, *Bunga Rampai Sastra Bugis: Bacaan sejarah Sulawesi Selatan* [*Anthology of Bugis Literature: Historical texts of South Sulawesi*], Departemen Pendidikan dan Kebudayaan, Proyek Penerbitan Buku Sastra Indonesia dan Daerah, Jakarta.

Crawfurd, J. 1820, *History of the Indian Archipelago*, 3 vols, Archibald Constable & Co., Edinburgh.

Cummings, W. 2002, *Making Blood White: Historical transformations in early modern Makassar*, University of Hawai`i Press, Honolulu.

Cummings, W. 2010, *The Makassar Annals*, Bibliotheca Indonesica 35, KITLV Press, Leiden.

Cummings, W.P. 2007, *A Chain of Kings: The Makassarese chronicles of Gowa and Talloq*, Bibliotheca Indonesica 33, KITLV Press, Leiden. doi.org/10.26530/OAPEN_376974.

Druce, S.C. 2009, *The Lands West of the Lakes: A history of the Ajattappareng kingdoms of South Sulawesi 1200 to 1600 CE*, Verhandelingen van het Koninklijk Instituut voor Taal-, Land- en Volkenkunde 261, KITLV Press, Leiden. doi.org/10.26530/OAPEN_381395.

Forrest, T. 1792, *A Voyage from Calcutta to the Mergui Archipelago*, J. Robson, London.

Fox, J.J. 2008, 'Installing the "outsider" inside: The exploration of an epistemic Austronesian cultural theme and its social significance', *Indonesia and the Malay World* 36(105): 201–16. doi.org/10.1080/13639810802267942.

Gaynor, J.L. 2016, *Intertidal History in Island Southeast Asia: Submerged genealogy & the legacy of coastal capture*, Southeast Asia Program Publications, Cornell University Press, Ithaca, NY. doi.org/10.7591/9780877272304.

Gervaise, N. 1701, *An Historical Description of the Kingdom of Macasar in the East Indies*, T. Leigh & D. Midwinter, London.

Gising, B. 2002, *Sejarah kerajaan Tanete* [*History of the Kingdom of Tanete*], No publisher, [?] Makassar.

Hamid, P. and Kartikasari, T. 1992–93, *Lontarak Tellumpoccoe*, Departemen Pendidikan dan Kebudayaan, Direktorat Jenderal Kebudayaan, Direktorat Sejarah dan Nilai Tradisional, Bagian Proyek Penelitian dan Pengkajian Kebudayaan Nusantara, Jakarta.

Hamonic, G. 1980, 'Du "langage des dieux" au langage de l'histoire: Quelques remarques à propos de l'historiographie bugis de Célèbes-sud [From the "language of the gods" to the language of history: Some remarks about the Bugis historiography of South Celebes]', *Archipel* 20: 303–16. doi.org/10.3406/arch.1980.1609.

Havelock, E.A. 1963, *Preface to Plato*, Blackwell, Oxford.

Henley, D. and Caldwell, I. 2008, 'Kings and covenants: Stranger-kings and social contract in Sulawesi', *Indonesia and the Malay World* 36(105): 269–91. doi.org/10.1080/13639810802268031.

Kern, R.A. 1929, 'Boegineesche scheppingsverhalen [Bugis creation stories]', in *Feestbundel Koninklijk Bataviaasch Genootschap van Kunsten en Wetenschappen [Celebratory Collection: On the occasion of its 150th anniversary, 1778–1928, Royal Batavian Society of Arts and Sciences]*, Kolff, Weltevreden, pp. 297–312.

Koolhof, S. 1999, 'The "La Galigo": A Bugis encyclopaedia and its growth', *Bijdragen tot de Taal-, Land- en Volkenkunde* 155: 362–87 [Republished in N. Rahman, A. Hukma and I. Anwar (eds), *La Galigo: Menelusuri jejak warisan sastra dunia* (*La Galigo: Exploring the traces of a legacy of world literature*), Universitas Hasanuddin/Kapubaten Barru, Makassar, 2003, pp. 4–33]. doi.org/10.1163/22134379-90003869.

Le Roux, C.C.F.M. 1930, 'De Rijksvlaggen van Bone [The state flags of Bone]', *Tijdschrift van het Koninklijk Batavaiaasch Genootschap voor Kunsten en Wetenschappen* 70(2–3): 1–64.

Macknight, C. (ed. and trans.) 2012, *Bugis and Makasar: Two short grammars*, South Sulawesi Studies 1, Karuda Press, Canberra.

Macknight, C.C. 1983, 'The rise of agriculture in South Sulawesi before 1600', *Review of Indonesian and Malaysian Affairs* 17: 92–116.

Macknight, C.C. 1984, 'The concept of a "work" in Bugis manuscripts', *Review of Indonesian and Malaysian Affairs* 18: 103–14.

Macknight, C.C. 1998, 'Notes on the chronicle of Boné', in K. Robinson and Mukhlis Paeni (eds), *Living through Histories: Culture, history and social life in South Sulawesi*, Department of Anthropology, Research School of Pacific and Asian Studies, The Australian National University and The National Archives of Indonesia, Canberra, pp. 43–54 [Translated as *Tapak-Tapak Waktu: Sejarah, kebudayaan, dan kehidupan sosial di Sulawesi Selatan*, Ininnawa, Makassar, 2005].

Macknight, C.C. 2000, 'South Sulawesi chronicles and their possible models', in A. Disney and E. Booth (eds), *Vasco da Gama and the Linking of Europe and Asia*, Oxford University Press, New Delhi, pp. 322–32.

Macknight, C.C. 2003, 'La Galigo in comparative perspectives', in N. Rahman, A. Hukma and I. Anwar (eds), *La Galigo: Menelusuri jejak warisan sastra dunia [La Galigo: Exploring the traces of a legacy of world literature]*, Universitas Hasanuddin/Kapubaten Barru, Makassar, pp. 349–72.

Macknight, C.C. 2016, 'The media of Bugis literacy: A coda to Pelras', in S.C. Druce (ed.), *Orality, Writing and History: The literature of the Bugis and Makasar of South Sulawesi, International Journal of Asia Pacific Studies* 12(Supp. 1): 53–72. doi.org/10.21315/ijaps2016.12.s1.4.

Macknight, C.C. and Caldwell, I.A. 2001, 'Variation in Bugis manuscripts', *Archipel* 61: 139–54. doi.org/10.3406/arch.2001.3616.

Matthes, B.F. 1864, *Boegineesche Chrestomathie* [*Bugis Chrestomathy*], Vol. 1, Makassar.

Matthes, B.F. 1872, *Boegineesche Chrestomathie* [*Bugis Chrestomathy*], Vols 2 and 3, Amsterdam.

Matthes, B.F. 1874a, *Boegineesch-Hollandsch Woordenboek met Hollandsch-Boegineesche Woordenlijst en verklaring van een tot opheldering bijgevoegden Ethnographischen Atlas* [*Bugis–Dutch Dictionary with Dutch–Bugis Glossary and Explanation of an Annexed Ethnographic Atlas*], M. Nijhoff, The Hague.

Matthes, B.F. 1874b, *Ethnographische Atlas, bevattende afbeeldingen van voorwerpen uit het leven en de huishouding der Boeginezen* [*Ethnographic Atlas, Containing Images of Objects from the Life and Households of the Bugis*], T. Brüggemann/C.A. Spin & Zoon, Amsterdam.

Matthes, B.F. 1875, *Kort verslag aangaande alle mij in Europa bekende Makassaarsche en Boeginesche handschriften* [*Short Report on All the Makasar and Bugis Manuscripts Known to Me in Europe*], Nederlandsch Bijbelgenootschap, Amsterdam.

Matthes, B.F. 1881, *Vervolg op het kort verslag aangaande alle mij in Europa bekende Makassaarsche en Boeginesche handschriften* [*Supplement to the Short Report on All the Makasar and Bugis Manuscripts Known to Me in Europe*], Nederlandsch Bijbelgenootschap, Amsterdam.

Matthes, B.F. 1885, 'Boegineesche en Makassaarsche legenden [Bugis and Makasar legends]', *Bijdragen tot de Taal-, Land- en Volkenkunde* 10: 1–64.

Millar, S.B. 1989, *Bugis Weddings: Rituals of social location in modern Indonesia*, Monograph No. 29, Center for South and Southeast Asia Studies, University of California at Berkeley, Berkeley.

Muhlis Hadrawi, Arwin Fajar, Basiah, Karmila, Abdi Mahesa, Suparman and Muhammad Hasbi 2018, *Lontara Sakke' Bone: Attoriolong ri Bone* [*The Complete Bone Manuscript: Chronicle of Bone*], Penerbit Ininnawa, Makassar.

Mukhlis Paeni and Others 2003, *Katalog induk naskah-naskah nusantara Sulawesi Selatan* [*Master Catalogue of Indonesian Manuscripts: South Sulawesi*], Arsip Nasional Republik Indonesia in collaboration with The Ford Foundation, Universitas Hasanuddin, Gadjah Mada University Press, [Makassar].

Niemann, G.K. 1883, *Geschiedenis van Tanette: Boeginesche text met aanteekeningen* [*History of Tanete: Bugis text with notes*], Nijhoff, The Hague.

Noorduyn, J. 1955, *Een achtteinde-eeuwse kroniek van Wadjo': Buginese historiographie* [*An Eighteenth-Century Chronicle of Wajo: Bugis Historiography*], Smits, The Hague.

Noorduyn, J. 1961, 'Some aspects of Macassar–Buginese historiography', in D.G.E. Hall (ed.), *Historians of South East Asia*, Oxford University Press, London, pp. 29–36.

Noorduyn, J. 1965, 'Origins of South Celebes historical writing', in Soedjatmoko (ed.), *An Introduction to Indonesian Historiography*, Cornell University Press, Ithaca, NY, pp. 137–55.

Noorduyn, J. 1983, 'De handelsrelaties van het Makassaarse rijk volgens de Notitie van Cornelis Speelman uit 1670 [The trade relations of the Makasar empire according to the memorandum of Cornelis Speelman from 1670]', *Nederlandse Historische Bronnen* 3: 97–121.

Nooy-Palm, H. 1986, *The Sa'dan-Toraja: A study of their social life and religion. Volume 2: Rituals of the east and west*, Verhandelingen van het Koninklijk Instituut voor Taal-, Land- en Volkenkunde 118, Foris Publications, Dordrecht.

Nur, M. Rafiuddin 2007, *Lontara'-na Soppeng dari kerajaan-kembar menuju kabupaten* [*Lontara' in the Soppeng Regency: From the royal twins to the district*], Rumah Ide, Makassar.

Palloge Petta Nabba, A. 2006, *Sejarah kerajaan tanah Bone (Masa raja pertama dan raja-raja kemudiannya sebelum masuknya Islam sampai terakhir)* [*History of the Kingdom of Bone (From the First King and Later Pre-Muslim Kings up to the Last*)], Yayasan Al Muallim, [Makassar]. [The cover suggests an earlier printing as well in 1990.]

Parry, A. (ed.) 1971, *The Making of Homeric Verse: The collected papers of Milman Parry*, Clarendon Press, Oxford.

Pelras, C. 1979, 'L'oral et l'écrit dans la tradition Bugis [The oral and the written in the Bugis tradition]', *Asie du Sud-est et Monde Insulindien* (*ASEMI*) 10: 271–97 [Reprinted, with minor alterations, in C. Pelras, *Explorations dans l'univers des Bugis: Un choix de trente-trois rencontres* (*Explorations in the World of the Bugis: A selection of thirty-three encounters*), Cahier d'Archipel 39, Paris, 2010, pp. 123–43. [There is an English translation: Pelras, C. 2016, 'Orality and writing among the Bugis', (trans. C.C. Macknight), in S.C. Druce (ed.), *Orality, Writing and History: The literature of the Bugis and Makasar of South Sulawesi*, *International Journal of Asia Pacific Studies* 12(Supp. 1): 13–51. doi.org/10.21315/ijaps2016.12.s1.3].

Pelras, C. 2000, 'Patron–client ties among the Bugis and Makassarese of South Sulawesi', in R. Tol, K. van Dijk and G. Acciaioli (eds), *Authority and Enterprise among the Peoples of South Sulawesi, Bijdragen tot de Taal-, Land- en Volkenkunde* 156: 393–432 [Reprinted in Pelras, C., *Explorations dans l'univers des Bugis: Un choix de trente-trois rencontres* (*Explorations in the World of the Bugis: A selection of thirty-three encounters*), Cahier d'Archipel 39, Paris, 2010, pp. 393–419]. doi.org/10.1163/22134379-90003833.

Perelaer, M.T.H. 1872, *De Bonische Expeditiën: Krijgsgebeurtenissen op Celebes in 1859 and 1860* [*The Bone Expeditions: The wars in Celebes in 1859 and 1860*], 2 vols, Kolff, Leiden.

Raffles, T.S. 1817, *The History of Java*, 2 vols, Black, Parbury & Allen and John Murray, London.

Ricklefs, M.C. and Voorhoeve, P. 1977, *Indonesian Manuscripts in Great Britain: A catalogue of manuscripts in Indonesian languages in British public collections*, Oxford University Press, London.

Robson, S. 1995, *Deśawarṇana (Nāgarakṛtāgama) by Mpu Prapañca*, KITLV Press, Leiden.

Sirk, Ü. 1996, *The Buginese Language of Traditional Literature*, Self-published, Moscow.

Skinner, C. 1963, *Sja'ir Perang Mengkasar (The Rhymed Chronicle of the Macassar War) by Entji' Amin*, Verhandelingen van het Koninklijk Instituut voor Taal-, Land- en Volkenkunde 40, Nijhoff, The Hague.

Stapel, F.W. 1922, *Het Bongaais verdrag* [*The Bongaya Treaty*], Wolters, Groningen.

Stapel, F.W. 1936, 'Cornelis Janszoon Speelman', *Bijdragen tot de taal-, land- en volkenkunde* 94(1). doi.org/10.1163/22134379-90001367.

Stavorinus, J.S. 1798, *Voyages to the East-Indies*, (trans. S.H. Wilcocke), 3 vols, G.G. & J. Robinson, London.

Teeuw, A. 1984, 'Indonesia as a "field of literary study": A case study—Genealogical narrative texts as an Indonesian literary genre', in P.E. de Josselin de Jong (ed.), *Unity in Diversity: Indonesia as a field of anthropological study*, Foris Publications, Dordrecht, pp. 38–59.

Tideman, J. 1908, 'De Toe Badjeng en de legende omtrent hun oorsprong [The Toe Badjeng and the legend about their origin]', *Bijdragen tot de Taal-, Land- en Volkenkunde* 60: 488–500. doi.org/10.1163/22134379-90001933.

Tol, R. 1990, *Een haan in oorlog: Toloqna Arung Labuaja* [*A Rooster at War: Toloqna Arung Labuaja*], Verhandelingen van het Koninklijk Instituut voor Taal-, Land- en Volkenkund 141, Foris Publications, Dordrecht.

Valentijn, F. 1858, *Oud en Nieuw Oost-Indië* [*Old and New East Indies*], (ed. S. Keijzer), H.C. Susan, The Hague.

van den Brink, H. 1943, *Dr Benjamin Frederik Matthes: Zijn leven en arbeid in dienst van het Nederlandsch Bijbelgenootschap* [*Dr Benjamin Frederik Matthes: His life and work in the service of the Dutch Bible Society*], Nederlandsch Bijbelgenootschap, Amsterdam.

van Hoëvell, W.R. 1854, 'Bijdragen tot de geschiedenis van Celebes [Contributions to the history of Celebes]', *Tijdschrift voor Nederlandsch Indië* 16(2): 149–86, 213–53.

Volkman, T.A. 1985, *Feasts of Honour: Ritual and change in the Toraja highlands*, Illinois Studies in Anthropology No. 16, University of Illinois Press, Urbana.

Warner, R. 1954, *Thucydides: History of the Peloponnesian War*, Penguin Books, Harmondsworth, UK.

Yule, H. and Burnell, A.C. 1903, *Hobson-Jobson: A glossary of colloquial Anglo-Indian words and phrases, and of kindred terms, etymological, historical, geographical and discursive*, Routledge & Kegan Paul, London.

Index

Persons with a Bugis name are referenced in a main entry, usually under their personal name—that is, the name after La or Wé. This main entry also lists other names or titles. Entries under these names or titles refer back to the main entry. All references to a particular individual are listed in the main entry.

The title of *Arung* or ruler is usually followed by a placename, which is used for the relevant entry with the title abbreviated to *Ar*. Thus, separate, but adjacent, entries are made for the place and the person.

Page numbers in **bold type** refer to maps and figures.

www.ingramcontent.com/pod-product-compliance
Lightning Source LLC
Chambersburg PA
CBHW041755010726
47507CB00015B/376

9781760463571